LIVING FROM THE
PRESENCE
INTERACTIVE MANUAL

LIVING FROM THE
PRESENCE
INTERACTIVE MANUAL

HEIDI BAKER
with ROLLAND BAKER

DESTINY IMAGE® PUBLISHERS, INC.

P.O. Box 310, Shippensburg, PA 17257-0310

"Promoting Inspired Lives."

This book and all other Destiny Image and Destiny Image Fiction books are available at Christian bookstores and distributors worldwide.

Cover design by Eileen Rockwell
Interior design by Terry Clifton

For more information on foreign distributors, call 717-532-3040.

Reach us on the Internet: www.destinyimage.com.

ISBN 13 TP: 978-0-7684-1237-6
ISBN eBook: 978-0-7684-4270-0

For Worldwide Distribution, Printed in the U.S.A.
1 2 3 4 5 6 7 8 / 21 20 19 18 17

CONTENTS

INTRODUCTION

Then Moses said to him, "If your Presence does not go with us, do not send us up from here. How will anyone know that you are pleased with me and with your people unless you go with us? What else will distinguish me and your people from all the other people on the face of the earth?"
—EXODUS 33:15-16

THIS STUDY, *LIVING FROM THE PRESENCE*, IS ABOUT ONE OF THE MOST foundational elements of the Christian life—how to live under the active, continuous influence of the Spirit of God.

When someone first receives Jesus as Savior and Lord, unfortunately this person is often inundated with a list of "to dos." Now that you are "saved," you need to: 1) join this new believer's class, 2) attend this Bible study, 3) go to this conference, 4) follow these rules, 5) find a discipleship mentor, 6) join a small group, etc. Many of these "new believer" assignments are positive, for sure. They are meant to lead to growth and maturity. The problem is this: when discipleship and spiritual development are absent from a vibrant lifestyle of Holy Spirit encounter, what's meant for good can become destructive.

There are Christians across the earth who are well-trained, well-learned, and well-educated. Their theology is sound and they are actively involved in all kinds of ministry projects. Yet some of these people are the hungriest of all. Information cannot fill the hunger, and activity cannot satisfy the thirst.

What's the secret? *Living from His Presence.*

Quickly return to the conversation between Moses and God in Exodus 33—a foundational portion of Scripture for the study you are preparing to begin. What sets apart the people of God?

What distinguishes them, making them unique from *all the other people on the face of the earth?* It's not our churches—size or structure. It's not our programs. It's not our music or media. It's not our small groups. It's not any of these secondary matters, which are positive and healthy in their place. What sets you apart is the One who lives within you.

The Christian life is not a journey of learning or doing; it's a lifelong, interactive relationship with One called God, the Holy Spirit. In the pages and sessions to come, prepare your heart to receive a reset. A walk with God is not about information or activity; it's about living from the Presence of the One who has made you His dwelling place!

How to Use the Interactive Manual

TO GET THE MOST OUT OF THIS EXPERIENCE, IT IS STRONGLY RECOMMENDED that you work through this manual and its interactive exercises in conjunction with the *Living from the Presence* curriculum resources. The curriculum can be done as a small group, a class, or an individual experience.

You would first watch the video sessions, and then work through the appropriate manual exercises throughout the week. The schedule would involve you working through one session and its interactive exercises each week.

Remember: this resource is for you. Interact with it honestly. Fill up the blank pages and journal space with your thoughts and interactions with the Holy Spirit. It is not intended to simply provide you with information—it is being presented to you as a vehicle to help you experience the Presence of God in a whole new dimension.

If you desire a more exhaustive teaching on the topic of living from the Presence of God, it is recommended that you watch the curriculum video sessions in conjunction with going through the interactive manual.

SUMMARY

You will receive an introductory summary of each session.

INTERACTIVE DISCUSSION QUESTIONS

You can answer these discussion questions individually by writing in the space provided or in a small group/Bible study class through oral discussion and conversation. If you go through the sessions with a group or class, it is still recommended that you personally work through each of the Interactive Discussion Questions on your own time so you can fully process the concepts you are learning.

ACTIVATION EXERCISES

These exercises can be done either in a group setting or by an individual.

If the Activation Segment is being done in a group or class setting, it is recommended that the group leader set aside an appropriate amount of time at the end of the class for both the activation segment and questions/answers from those who want to share about their experience during the segment. This is where the information learned in each session will be processed and implemented.

DEVOTIONAL READINGS

These entries are intended to help reinforce the concepts you learn while watching the video sessions, although they can be read and interacted with outside of watching the sessions.

Session
1

BUILDING YOUR THEOLOGY OF GOD'S PRESENCE

Rolland Baker

SUMMARY

It's important for you to understand that the Presence of God is not a thing; it's not an additional member of the Trinity—Father, Son, Spirit, and Presence. The Presence of God is a Person, and in order for you to experience His Presence in the measure that's available, it's important for you to establish a solid theological foundation for *who* God is.

Even though more learning is not the key to a life saturated in the Presence of God, there are certain truths we need to build our lives upon. Truth is the gateway to experience. Before you can pursue Bible experience, you need to first have a foundation of Bible truth, for Bible truth is what establishes your appetite for Bible experience.

There are many in the body of Christ, particularly in Spirit-empowered circles, who passionately pursue experience, and rightly so. Then, there are streams and denominations that uphold the supremacy of God's written Word, *truth*. They are equally as correct. The problem is when truth and experience exist separated from one another. This produces cultures where people become puffed up with knowledge (all *truth*) or people move beyond Bible parameters and pursue experiences that are not the will of God (all *experience*).

To fully experience God, it's best to start with a foundation of truth. Then, based on the parameters of that truth, you can press in to actually experience the reality that truth claims is available.

INTERACTIVE QUESTIONS

1. What does "freedom in the house" look like? How do you understand *yourself* to be the "house" of God?

_____

_____

_____

_____

_____

_____

_____

_____

_____

2. Discuss: Why do you think it's important to have a correct theology of God?

_____

_____

_____

_____

_____

_____

_____

_____

3. How does your theology and understanding of who God is actually determine what you experience of His Presence?

_____

_____

_____

_____

_____

_____

_____

_____

_____

Whatever you think about God is your theology. #livefromthepresence

4. Read Proverbs 9:10. How is the *fear of the Lord* connected with how we experience His Presence? Explain your understanding of what the fear of the Lord is and how it's so beneficial.

    The fear of the Lord is the beginning of wisdom, and knowledge of the Holy One is understanding.

_____

_____

_____

_____

_____

_____

_____

_____

_____

_____

5. What does salvation mean to you? What do you think it means to different people? Why do you think it's important to know what Jesus saved you from?

_____

_____

_____

_____

_____

_____

_____

_____

_____

Everything you experience
about God impacts the way
you think about Him.

6. What does the following statement mean to you: "*God is in control*"? How does your view
of God being in control positively impact your life and walk with the Lord?

_____

_____

_____

_____

_____

_____

_____

_____

7. Discuss the following statement: "When God moved in, Heaven began" (based on John
17:3).

*Now this is eternal life: that they know you, the only true God, and Jesus Christ,
whom you have sent.*

_____

_____

_____

_____

_____

_____

_____

_____

Heaven is *both* a place that we go to and a reality that begins *now* in our hearts. #livefromthepresence

ACTIVATION EXERCISES

Meditate on the truth that *you* are the temple of God. You are the house of the Holy Spirit!

In whatever context you have available to you, put this truth into practice.

Group Activation

As a group, focus on the Person and Presence of the Spirit dwelling within them. If need be, use an atmosphere of quiet reflection and soft worship—if possible. Sometimes, we allow worship to distract us from the fact that God lives within us.

Individual Activation

Focus inward—not on yourself, but on Christ in you. "Christ in you" is possible because the Holy Spirit has made you His home, His preferred dwelling place. Ask God to increase your awareness of the closeness of His Presence. Even though Heaven is your destination one day, Heaven can also be your experience *today* through the abiding Presence of the Spirit.

Day 1

THERE IS FREEDOM

Now the Lord is the Spirit, and where the Spirit
of the Lord is, there is freedom.
—2 CORINTHIANS 3:17

WE VISITED TIBET, AND AS YOU MAY KNOW THERE ARE A VARIETY OF RELIGIONS practiced there. Rolland actually grew up in China and in Tibet and was around Buddhist temples and in the midst of the culture. In the temples, they burn candles and incense. The leaders wear robes and have processions. There is a lot of repetitive chanting that involves beads. They learn self-discipline and asceticism, training themselves to function exactly and perfectly according to the rules. When you think about it, we have a lot of that in Christianity—repetitious prayers, robes, self-help, etc.

Buddhists also have prayer wheels where they place a roll of written mantras, and supposedly as it spins it is releasing the prayers into the universe. In some Christian circles, they too have a type of prayer wheel. Repeating the same prayers over and over becomes rote and many times meaningless. Although Jesus offered His disciples a model of prayer—the Lord's Prayer—it is only to be used as a guide to prayer. Our relationship with God should be free; our communication with Him personal and intimate.

The Holy Spirit brings freedom—freedom to worship, pray, and praise God in your own special, unique way. Where can you truly be completely free in your enjoyment of Jesus? In the shower when no one else is home, perhaps? You can't be totally free to enjoy Jesus at school, and not in your cubicle at work—not on the bus or the subway. You're not free at the factory or the shopping mall or a restaurant. Unfortunately, sometimes you can't even enjoy Him at church!

We need a place where we can be completely free, unglued, able to receive and express all that the Holy Spirit wants us to experience. We can only do that when our spirits are connected with God's Spirit—the Holy Spirit. That place starts right where you are, right now. Any place can become a place of encounter because the Spirit of God has made *you* His home!

DEVOTIONAL READING

Read Galatians 5:1: "*It is for freedom that Christ has set us free. Stand firm, then, and do not let yourselves be burdened again by a yoke of slavery.*" What things in your life are keeping you "yoked"? How can you break free of these entanglements and go deeper in your relationship with God?

Day

2

YOUR THEOLOGY OF GOD

What comes into our minds when we think about God
is the most important thing about us.
—A.W. TOZER, *The Knowledge of the Holy*

WHATEVER YOU THINK ABOUT GOD IS YOUR THEOLOGY, AND IT AFFECTS HOW you feel about Him in everything you do. Everything you experience in God affects everything you think about Him. Your head and your heart are connected, actually.

Theology is not God. The Word of God is not God—it's a love letter from God, but it's not God. I'm not in love with the Bible; I'm in love with God. I'm not in love with prayer; I'm in love with God. I'm not in love with worship; I'm in love with the One I worship. Yet, we do need to think about theology because if you think wrong things about God, it's going to hinder you. It's going to block you from having access to all that God wants to give you. It's going to stop you from moving forward in your destiny. It's going to undo what God has done. Theology is actually important—what you think about God is important.

DEVOTIONAL READING

In the story of the woman at the well in John 4, she asks Jesus where God should be worshiped—on Mt. Gerizim or Jerusalem? Jesus responds by explaining that the place of worship is irrelevant.

> *"Woman," Jesus replied, "believe me, a time is coming when you will worship the Father neither on this mountain nor in Jerusalem. You Samaritans worship what you do not know; we worship what we do know, for salvation is from the Jews. Yet a time is coming and has now come when the true worshipers will worship the Father in the Spirit and in truth, for they are the kind of worshipers the Father seeks. God is spirit, and his worshipers must worship in the Spirit and in truth"* (John 4:21-24).

Jesus is giving her information about the nature of God. What are some other aspects of God's nature and where are they found in Scripture?

Day
3

THE GRACE OF GOD IN JESUS

*The fear of the Lord is the beginning of knowledge, but
fools despise wisdom and instruction.*
—**Proverbs 1:7**

WHAT IS THE BEGINNING OF WISDOM? THE FEAR OF THE LORD. "*THE FEAR OF THE Lord is the beginning of knowledge*" (Prov. 1:7). I dug deeply into the Hebrew and Greek to find the real meaning of *fear*, and I found out that it actually means fear as well as awe, reverence, respect, honor, and devotion. The bottom line—don't upset God.

That statement immediately raises all kinds of questions, including: Can we really upset God? Or did He pour out all His wrath on Jesus 2,000 years ago, so now He's not upset about anything anymore? Does fearing the Lord mean we have to be afraid of Him? There are many more questions that come to mind. The "fear of the Lord" has always been an interesting phrase.

People I know who have had incredibly detailed, multiple visions of hell tell me that those experiences changed their lives more than anything that has ever happened to them. I don't think you hear enough about hell. Eternal separation from God is real—and should be taken seriously. You need to know what Jesus saves you from. You need to know what He thinks of sin. You need to know how bad sin is. You need to know that Jesus told the truth when He said that even calling somebody a fool (looking down on somebody, thinking somebody is worse than you) puts you in danger of going to hell. Jesus says, *"But I tell you that anyone who is angry with a brother or sister will be subject to judgment. Again, anyone who says to a brother or sister, 'Raca,' is answerable to the court. And anyone who says, 'You fool!' will be in danger of the fire of hell"* (Matt. 5:22).

Even the slightest mistake, even the slightest failing, the slightest little sin disqualifies you from Heaven and brings the wrath of God and hell down on you—*if it weren't for the grace of God in Jesus.*

PRESENCE PRAYER

Father, I know I didn't deserve Your grace. I could not earn it; I cannot earn it today. Even the slightest mistake, the smallest error on my part makes me fit for eternal punishment. Thank You for the precious blood of Jesus that saved me and saves me from Your wrath against sin.

Give me a vision of what I have been saved from so I value my salvation more than ever!

MEDITATE

Meditate on the following Scriptures:

I feared the anger and wrath of the Lord, *for he was angry enough with you to destroy you. But again the Lord listened to me* (Deuteronomy 9:19).

Now let **the fear of the Lord** *be on you. Judge carefully, for with the Lord our God there is no injustice or partiality or bribery* (2 Chronicles 19:7).

The fear of the Lord *is pure, enduring forever. The decrees of the Lord are firm, and all of them are righteous* (Psalm 19:9).

Through love and faithfulness sin is atoned for; through **the fear of the Lord** *evil is avoided* (Proverbs 16:6).

Since, then, we know what it is to **fear the Lord***, we try to persuade others* (2 Corinthians 5:11).

Day

4

IS GOD IN CONTROL?

Then Jesus said, "Come to me, all of you who are weary and carry heavy burdens, and I will give you rest. Take my yoke upon you. Let me teach you, because I am humble and gentle at heart, and you will find rest for your souls. For my yoke is easy to bear, and the burden I give you is light."
—MATTHEW 11:28-30 NLT

IF OUR PRAYERS CONSIST OF TELLING GOD WHAT TO DO, WE WILL FIND OUR relationship with the Father becoming strained and distorted. It is much better to come to Him realizing we are sinners. We are not equal partners with God. We need God, the great I AM, not an equal partner. We need Somebody who can absolutely fix us, the One who has control, who can change hearts, finish what He began in us, and is able to present us before the throne without fault with great joy in His presence. We need Almighty God—the one we depend on every day in Africa. Without Him we could never exist with all the crises we encounter. We dump all our problems and issues on Him every night when we go to bed, because He invites us to.

When we press into God's Presence seeking intimacy with Him, if we have some seriously wrong ideas about Him, our relationship will be tainted and stymied. For example, if we think we're in a bargaining position, if we think we have any control over Him whatsoever, if we think that He needs our advice, if we think that we know ourselves better than He knows us, if we think that He's sort of helpless unless we provide Him with our input and our company and our hands and feet, then our relationship with Him is going to be distorted.

See God for who He is and respond to Him accordingly! This will change everything.

PRESENCE PRAYER

Gracious and loving heavenly Father, I come before You today acknowledging You as the great I AM. Change my heart; finish what You started in me. I need You in everything! There is no part of my life that is not in desperate need of You. I need Your holiness, Your righteousness, Your faithfulness, Your mercy and loving-kindness, Your love. I need everything about You. I need You, God.

REFLECT

Reflect on the following Scriptures:

Genesis 22:13-14: *Jehovah Jireh*—The Lord will provide

Exodus 15:26: *Jehovah Rapha*—The Lord who heals

Exodus 17:8-15: *Jehovah Nissi*—The Lord our Banner

Judges 6:24: *Jehovah Shalom*—The Lord our Peace

Psalm 23:1: *Jehovah Ra-ah*—The Lord my Shepherd

Jeremiah 23:6: *Jehovah-Tsidkenu*—The Lord our Righteousness

Ezekiel 48:35: *Jehovah-Shammah*—The Lord is present

Day 5

HEAVEN IN YOUR HEART

Now this is eternal life: that they know you, the only true
God, and Jesus Christ, whom you have sent.
—JOHN 17:3

HEAVEN IS A PLACE THAT WE GO TO ONE DAY; BUT IT ALSO A PLACE IN OUR hearts. We have a Kingdom, not made with human hands, being kept safe in Heaven waiting for us to be revealed when Jesus is revealed. All the outward stuff means nothing. The life message in our hearts is what counts. Although we know that God is all powerful, being fallible human beings we have twisted our thinking and effort and teaching and prayer into trying to figure out how to get God to do what we want Him to do. We need things. We need jobs. We need healing. We need friendship. We need stuff to happen. We need things to be fixed. We have all kinds of things going on and we need help, thinking, *Oh God, I need to go to a conference where I can learn how to get God to do what I think He needs to do for me. I will travel anywhere. I will give any amount of offering the preacher wants if I can just learn how to get God's power working for me.*

We receive e-mail all the time from people desperately sick and struggling with this and that; they're trying to find the key to their healing or breakthrough. They want to know where they can go and what they can do to get more power. Their health is a mess, their family is a mess, their country is in a big mess, and they are thinking, "*Maybe if I go to _ I can learn how to get God's power moving in the direction I think it should go.*"

There are seminars and books and teachings being offered today that cover thousands of topics concerning God. There are techniques and steps and ways to talk and pray and worship and do the supernatural and whatever. Sometimes I pray for God to have patience with us. We must acknowledge the fact that He is a great God—the only God in Heaven—and He will respond to His children who obey Him and follow His commandments. Living in and from His Presence will inevitably produce miracles. That you can rely on!

DEVOTIONAL READINGS

Take time to read these verses, reflecting on the relationship between God the Father and Jesus the Son, noting Jesus' complete dependence on the Father.

John 8:27-28: In these verses we see Jesus' great dependence on God the Father.

John 5:36: The Father was where Jesus found His strength.

John 10:30: Here we see perfect unity between Father and Son.

Notes

Session
2

DELIGHTING IN HIS MIRACLE-WORKING PRESENCE

Rolland Baker

SUMMARY

The joy of the Lord is a gift that flows from intimacy with the Giver. Joy is a fruit of the Spirit and the outcome of the Christian life; it is what you get when you get Jesus. His very Presence brings delight (see John 15:11). As we live in His glorious Presence, joy will bubble out of us in an unprecedented manner until it becomes a river gushing from the rushing waters of His love. Our delight in God is a natural reaction to His Presence and an expression of His Kingdom. It is our strength (see Neh. 8:10). Make no mistake about it—when you experience the joy down in your heart, you will be excited about sharing it with whomever you meet. As His love flows from you, you will find yourself longing desperately to go to the lost and broken with His miracle-working Presence. God is calling out to you every day, inviting you into His Presence. If you wait there with Him, when the time is right He will send you out. And when you go, you will mount up on wings of eagles, soaring with Him. God is calling you to live your life in intimacy with Jesus, fearlessly and passionately manifesting His glory, producing fruit in every season.

Jesus is a priceless Lover, and it will cost you everything to love Him, but oh the joy you will receive in return! Fall into His arms today. Delight in His Presence.

With your hand of love is upon my life, you impart a Father's blessing to me. This is just too wonderful, deep, and incomprehensible! ...Wherever I go, your hand will guide me; your strength will empower me. It's impossible to disappear from you or to ask the darkness to hide me; for your presence is everywhere bringing light into my night! There is no such thing as darkness with you. The night, to you, is as bright as the day (Psalm 139:5-6,10-12 TPT).

INTERACTIVE QUESTIONS

1. What is *your* natural reaction to the Presence of God?

_____

_____

_____

_____

_____

_____

_____

_____

_____

_____

2. Discuss: How is your reaction an expression of His Kingdom?

_____

_____

_____

_____

_____

_____

_____

_____

3. How is God daily inviting you into His Presence? What does His invitation look like for you? Describe your response to His invitation.

_____

_____

_____

_____

_____

_____

_____

_____

4. Read First Peter 1:13-16. *"For it is written, 'Be holy, because I am holy.'"* (1 Pet. 1:16). Explain your understanding of what it means to be holy. How can we become holy?

_____

_____

_____

_____

_____

_____

_____

_____

_____

_____

5. Based on Psalm 1 and other Scriptures, what does it means to bear fruit in every season?

    What delight comes to those who follow God's ways! …Bearing fruit in every season of their lives. They are never dry, never fainting, ever blessed, ever prosperous (Psalm 1:1,3 TPT).

_____

_____

_____

_____

_____

_____

_____

_____

_____

6. How do you describe intimacy with the Lord?

_____

_____

_____

_____

_____

_____

_____

_____

ACTIVATION EXERCISES

Meditate on the truth that the joy of the Lord is your strength. He is your glory-song!

Take time now to come into His Presence.

Group Activation

Draw away from any distractions and get alone with God in an atmosphere conducive to listening and reflection. When you come back together, if you feel led, share your meditations. Once the time of sharing is finished, join together for a few minutes of joyous spontaneous worship.

Individual Ativation

Eliminate distractions. Find a quiet place where you can be totally alone. Allow the Lord to invite you into His Presence. Ask Him to fill you with His joy. As His joy comes upon you, allow yourself to express this joy. Sing, dance, laugh with Him! Let yourself be overcome as you delight in His Presence.

Day
1

MARKED BY JOY

*Enter into His gates with thanksgiving, and into His courts
with praise. Be thankful to Him, and bless His name.*
—Psalm 100:4 NKJV

GOD IS INVITING YOU INTO HIS PRESENCE DAILY. ARE YOU RESPONDING positively to His invitation?

FILLED WITH HIM

I believe God is saying to you right now, "I'm calling you this day to go low, to go slow, to live lean. When you do, I will place in you a heart of compassion that will burn so brightly that it will change your life."

"I will fill you with Myself," says the Lord, "and as I fill you with Myself, you will be full of oil. You will burn for Me and not burn out."

"You will live a life burning for Me," says the Lord, "for I am calling you not to a small amount of oil, not to a little bitty bit of Presence. I'm calling you to a *lifetime* of My Presence, a life lived in intimacy with Jesus, a holy life manifesting the glory of God, a life that is fearless, a life that is passionate, a life with purpose, a life with destiny, a life marked by fire," says the Lord, "a life marked by holiness. Make no mistake about it—I have marked you for joy!"

Back in the day, the Lord said, *"And you shall command the children of Israel that they bring you pure oil of pressed olives for the light, to cause the lamp to burn continually"* (Exod. 27:20 NKJV). Today, it is God's will that through Jesus Christ's sacrifice and the Presence of the Holy Spirit you are filled with oil that will never run dry. His Presence keeps the fire of your spirit burning for Him continually as you work to advance His Kingdom on earth as it is in Heaven.

Therefore, since we are receiving a kingdom that cannot be shaken, let us be thankful, and so worship God acceptably with reverence and awe, for our "God is a consuming fire" (Hebrews 12:28-29).

PRESENCE PRAYER

Swing wide you gates of righteousness and let me pass through, and I will enter into your presence to worship only you! I have found the gateway to God, the pathway to his presence for all his lovers! I will offer all my loving praise to you! (Psalm 118:19-21 TPT)

BIBLE STUDY

Read Second Corinthians 3:7-18, giving particular attention to verses 17-18.

Explain how New Covenant ministry as reflected in this passage differs from Old Covenant ministry regarding freedom and joy.

Day
2

HOLINESS

Make every effort to live in peace with everyone and to be
holy; without holiness no one will see the Lord.
—**Hebrews 12:14**

HOLINESS CAN BE A VAGUE TERM, BUT IT ACTUALLY MEANS TO EXHIBIT GENUINE goodness and righteousness, devoted to God's work, having a divine quality. Those attributes include an attitude of devotion to God. How holy are you? How holy do you want to be?

God is calling you to come and live in His presence, to come out and be separate. In Leviticus He says, *"You shall be holy, for I the Lord your God am holy"* (Lev. 19:2 NKJV). To be holy is to be set apart from the profane, from anything that is not of God. Instead, you are to consecrate yourself to that which is pure. How do you dedicate yourself to the things of God? A good place to begin is with the washing of the Word. In Ephesians, Paul uses the analogy of the relationship between husbands and wives to demonstrate how we, the bride of Christ, are to be presented to Christ *"as a radiant church, without stain or wrinkle or any other blemish, but holy and blameless"* (Eph. 5:27).

Do you desire to exhibit genuine goodness and righteousness? To be devoted to God's work? To have a divine quality about you? Do you desire to be devoted to God?

PRESENCE PRAYER

Almighty and everlasting God, come now and touch my lips and remove my wickedness. I invite your searching gaze into my heart. Examine me through and through; find out everything that may be hidden within me. Put me to the test and sift through all my anxious cares. See if there is any path of pain I'm walking on, and lead me back to your glorious, everlasting ways—the path that brings me back to you (Psalm 139:23-24 TPT).

BIBLE STUDY

Come quietly into the Lord's presence and read Isaiah 6:1-12. Reflect on Isaiah's response to the Lord in verse 8 and God's instructions to Isaiah in verses 9-10. What is your response to the holiness of God, the One who sits upon the throne among the seraphim?

Day
3

INTIMACY

*O God, you are my God; earnestly I seek you; my soul thirsts for you; my flesh
faints for you, as in a dry and weary land where there is no water. So I have
looked upon you in the sanctuary, beholding your power and glory. Because your
steadfast love is better than life, my lips will praise you. So I will bless you as
long as I live; in your name I will lift up my hands. My soul will be satisfied
as with fat and rich food, and my mouth will praise you with joyful lips.*
—PSALM 63:1-5 ESV

REAL INTIMACY

The joy of the Lord is a gift that flows from intimacy. Christ living inside of you is the greatest blessing we can have this side of Heaven. As you draw near to Him, He will draw near to you, to comfort you, direct you, guide you, and love you. In His Presence is fullness of joy!

You're not really in love with Jesus until He is everything to you. Life with Christ is not Jesus plus this, plus that, plus the other thing—not Jesus plus all the things He can give you. What if He doesn't give you anything in this life? What if you die a beggar in the streets? If you love Him, you end up with Jesus. You have an eternity with the one Lover you need. There's no human being who can take His place, not even one—not the best spouse, not the best family, not the best friends, not the best church, not the best team, not the best group, not the best ministry, not the best denomination. None of can equal Jesus, who is pure love, pure romance. True intimacy with Jesus leaves us with a desire for more. The more we know Him, the more we want to know Him. Like the apostle Paul, consider everything a loss in view of the surpassing value of knowing Christ Jesus, our Lord.

PRESENCE PRAYER

O Lord, may You find me today entering Your gates with thanksgiving and Your courts with praise, giving thanks and blessing Your holy name! For You, O Lord, are good and Your loving kindness is everlasting, Your faithfulness to all generations.

DEVOTIONAL READING

Immerse yourself in Psalm 27, giving particular attention to verses 4-5:

Here's the one thing I crave from God, the one thing I seek above all else: I want the privilege of living with him every moment in his house, finding the sweet loveliness of his face, filled with awe, delighting in his glory and grace. I want to live my life so close to him that he takes pleasure in my every prayer (Psalm 27:4 TPT).

Day
4

AN EXPRESSION OF
HIS KINGDOM

Don't store up treasures here on earth, where moths eat them and rust destroys
them, and where thieves break in and steal. Store your treasures in heaven,
where moths and rust cannot destroy, and thieves do not break in and steal.
Wherever your treasure is, there the desires of your heart will also be.
—MATTHEW 6:19-21 NLT

WHAT ARE THE DESIRES OF YOUR HEART? WHEN YOU *"TAKE DELIGHT IN THE*
Lord...he will give you your heart's desires" (Ps. 37:4 NLT). Have you taken time recently to sort
out what is important in your life—what your heart's desires are? Are your heart's desires an
expression of His Kingdom?

God's Kingdom is a Kingdom of love, a place ruled by the spiritual authority of the Most High. It is not a physical place. The reign of God is manifested first in our hearts as righteousness, peace, and joy that translate into His love. This spiritual reign in the life of the believer is meant to overflow as we lift up His name in praise and joyfully do His will on earth as it is in Heaven.

When we are filled with joy, we pray about everything; God becomes our "go-to guy" for interceding for others, asking for guidance, and praising and thanking Him for all that's good in our lives. There is no need to worry about this or that; when we are considerate in our relationships at home, at work, at church, wherever we are, God's peace will envelop us, dispelling worry and stress. Instead of walking around with frowns, we can smile and laugh daily as His blessing of joy rains down over us. Did you know that fifteen minutes of laughter equals two hours of sleep for your body? Laughter is actually the only thing I've heard medical doctors say recreates brain cells. We need laughter. The church needs to embrace the joy of God's Kingdom. To live in and from the Presence with joy expresses the Kingdom. How many people would want to follow a Jesus who is always complaining or sad or worried? Not many, if any.

BIBLE STUDY

Read Matthew 10:7 and Mark 1:15. How does Jesus say that we are to be an expression of His Kingdom? Are the desires of your heart an expression of His Kingdom?

Day 5

BEARING FRUIT IN EVERY SEASON

That you may live a life worthy of the Lord and please him
in every way: bearing fruit in every good work.
—COLOSSIANS 1:10

AS YOU FIND YOURSELF LIVING IN GOD'S PRESENCE, YOUR SPIRIT WILL FLOW IN the glory of His joy and love and you will "find fruit in every season," says the Lord. In every season there will be fruitfulness in and out of natural seasons, and there will be the rain of His Presence in and out of the natural season. When the rain of His Presence reigns in your heart, you will desire to go into the darkest, driest places, to go to the lowest and the least, knowing there's always enough of God for you and everyone you touch in His name. There is no season to the glorious power of God. The grace of God in your heart is always available, no matter the circumstances.

As sons and daughters, we have this great inheritance purchased by His blood. As you renew your mind in relationship with God, you will discover what He desires to do in you and through you. In order to be fruitful, we must first be filled—filled with the knowledge of God's will in the power of His Holy Spirit. That's the equation—relationship with God yields knowledge of His will, releasing fruit for the Kingdom.

PRESENCE PRAYER

Father God, fill me with the knowledge of Your perfect will through wisdom and understanding from Your Holy Spirit, so that I may live a life worthy of You, pleasing You in every way and bearing fruit in every good work to the glory of Your name!

SCRIPTURE REFLECTION

Read John 15:1-8 and Revelation 1:20. Reflect on how the branch of the Lord is now Christ living in you, giving particular attention to verse 8: *"This is to my Father's glory, that you bear much fruit, showing yourselves to be my disciples."*

Notes

Session
3

FINDING THE PERSON BEHIND THE PRESENCE

Rolland Baker

"Let not the wise boast of their wisdom or the strong boast of their strength or the rich boast of their riches, but let the one who boasts boast about this: that they have the understanding to know me, that I am the Lord, who exercises kindness, justice and righteousness on earth, for in these I delight," declares the Lord.
—JEREMIAH 9:23-24

SUMMARY

From being *in* His presence, we can live *from* His presence—going *out* of the house, *out* of the church, *out* of Bible studies and going *into* the marketplace, the workplace, the mission fields, the hospitals, the retirement centers, and every place God urges us to go.

As we discover the Person of Jesus behind His Presence, the legalism of religion gives way to the freedom of walking in holiness. Some think that holiness means you have to stash yourself away from life lest its temptations lure you into unholy living. Actually, quite the opposite is true. When you find the Person behind the Presence, you become so full that it is impossible to keep to yourself. You become so full of Him that fleshly things hold no sway with you. When you experience His Presence in the secret place, it will naturally burst forth from you into your everyday reality. You won't just go forth, you'll *run* forth into the world full of passion to share the Good News because it will be impossible to keep it to yourself.

INTERACTIVE QUESTIONS

1. The beloved disciple John found his identity not in knowing Jesus but in Jesus' love. How would you go about following John's example to the heart of Jesus?

2. What does it look like to live out your relationship with God from a place of Presence?

_____

_____

_____

_____

_____

_____

_____

_____

_____

3. Explain the upside-down nature of the Kingdom of God as Jesus explained it in the Gospel of Matthew. Give three examples.

_____

_____

_____

_____

_____

_____

_____

_____

4. Describe how you faithfully represent Jesus' upside-down Kingdom?

_____

_____

_____

_____

_____

_____

_____

_____

5. How would you define God's sovereignty? What does it mean to honor God's sovereignty?

_____

_____

_____

6. In light of Paul's prayer for the Ephesians, how are we made complete in God?

7. Describe what it looks like to "find Jesus."

_____

_____

_____

_____

_____

_____

_____

_____

_____

ACTIVATION EXERCISES

Read Daniel 6:10-23 and Romans 15:13.

According to Romans 15:13, where does our hope come from? How is our hope related to our level of trust? Explain your answers from a New Covenant perspective versus the Old Covenant.

Do you just want a relationship Jesus that is sweet and comforting, or are you willing to trust Him even when it means turning your life upside down?

Group Activation

Reflect on the scriptures and questions in the Activation Exercise, and then share your answers with a willingness to be vulnerable.

Individual Activation

Think on your level of trust in God, reflecting on how vulnerable you feel at the prospect of trusting Him to the point of turning your life upside down. Explain how your trust is based on either Old Covenant thinking or New Covenant thinking.

Day
1

PRESENTS OR PRESENCE

You have made known to me the path of life; you will fill me with
joy in your presence, with eternal pleasures at your right hand.
—Psalm 16:11

LIVING FROM THE PRESENCE MEANS GOING WHERE GOD SENDS YOU, SHARING
the Good News of the gospel with all who will listen. It means pursuing His holy and glorious
Presence, not His presents.

Do you realize it's possible to be more enamored by somebody's *presents* than that person's *presence?* I have been seated in a room where the speaker had a lot of power and as a result of that power I felt electric shock bolts and smelled fragrances and saw sparkles in the air and feathers falling. I could feel the power and voltage in the room—but that doesn't mean I knew the speaker. That doesn't mean I had a close or intimate relationship with the speaker. We can get all excited by phenomena in a Spirit-filled meeting where the Presence of God is very strong. We can be knocked down by Holy Spirit, but that doesn't mean we're in love with Him. I can be in somebody's presence and the power may make the person's presence very, very palatable, very felt, very obvious, but that doesn't mean I'm in a close relationship with that person.

It is vitally important for Christians to make this crucial distinction: *we are not in love with a person's powerful presence—we are in love with Him from whose Presence we are living.* There is a huge difference between the two. I would rather be out in the dark in the parking lot, sitting quietly in the grass somewhere with Jesus than in a meeting where all kinds of fantastic, amazing things are happening. If there is no intimate relationship, there is no Presence.

PRESENCE PRAYER

Precious Jesus, let Your presence go with me always and everywhere. Make known to me the path of life so that I may find fullness of joy in Your Presence and pleasures at Your right hand. Teach me how to abide in Your love regardless of circumstances.

BIBLE STUDY

Read Matthew 28:16-20. How does this passage demonstrate an aspect of what it means to "live from His Presence"?

Day 2

HAVE YOU FOUND JESUS?

For I know the thoughts that I think toward you, says the Lord, thoughts of peace and not of evil, to give you a future and a hope. Then you will call upon Me and go and pray to Me, and I will listen to you. And you will seek Me and find Me, when you search for Me with all your heart.
—JEREMIAH 29:11-13 NKJV

IF YOU WERE TO ASK MOST CHRISTIANS, "HAVE YOU FOUND JESUS?" I THINK A great many of them would say, "Yes." But in what sense, to what degree, and in what way have we found Jesus? In some Christian circles, Jesus is not talked about very much at all. Why not? Perhaps because He has been relegated to the past, as someone who lived 2,000 years ago, and whatever He came to do is done. He paid the price; now we just need to go out and get empowered. It seems that some Christians think their faith is only all about being empowered by the Holy Spirit. Then there are those who bypass Holy Spirit altogether and just go straight for the Father. I know of whole conferences where Jesus is hardly mentioned, if at all. I believe it's time to call for another reformation.

Church ministry is not a corporation or a political election. It's not a popularity contest. It's not an athletic event. It's not competition. Church ministry is God's Kingdom, and everything in the Kingdom is upside down. There is no pressure—none, zero, no compulsion whatsoever. Freedom in the house of God means that you're not trying to get somewhere or achieve something. You're not trying to make something out of your life, and you're not trying to take ownership of your life. You don't need worldly success. You need a perfect Lover who can transform you into exactly what He wants, into exactly what makes you happiest. Finding Jesus is exactly what your heart wanted all along, what your heart is designed for.

SCRIPTURE REFLECTION

Read Psalm 15. A study of Scripture tells us that King David likely wrote this as instruction to those who desired access to God. We now have access to God through Jesus. How is what David speaks about in this Psalm a reflection of finding Jesus?

Day

3

SEEK HIM WITH ALL YOUR HEART

RECENTLY I HAVE HAD THE OPPORTUNITY TO READ ABOUT MANY OF THE GREAT spiritual mystics in history. I found a similar thread running through each of their stories—that life can actually be very simple in Jesus alone.

In First Corinthians 2:1-4, Paul was challenged to the limit, causing him to say he would focus on nothing else but Jesus. At another time, Paul wrote: *"But I am afraid that just as Eve was deceived by the serpent's cunning, your minds may somehow be led astray from your sincere and pure devotion to Christ"* (2 Cor. 11:3). Paul's formula for living was very simple—the purity and simplicity of devotion to Christ. That's it! Life is not to be about loving Jesus by doing this and doing that to remind Him that we are still here. The sole purpose of our existence is Him! Loving Him is why we live. Jesus gives you the reason to get up in the morning—just to love Him! When you're in love, you seek your lover with all your heart.

PRESENCE PRAYER

O Lord, our Lord, how majestic is Your name in all the earth! You have set Your glory above the heavens. I will praise You today with all my heart. I will tell of Your wonders and gladly rejoice in You, singing praises to Your name. Apart from You I have no good thing. O Lord, You are worthy of all praise!

SCRIPTURE REFLECTION

Read and reflect on Matthew 6:33: *"But seek first his kingdom and his righteousness, and all these things will be given to you as well."*

Day
4

HONORING GOD'S SOVEREIGNTY

GOD'S SOVEREIGNTY IS NOT TO BE QUESTIONED; HONORING HIS POSITION AS
the all-powerful sovereign God is our privilege, pleasure, and joy. Are you close enough to God
for Him to demand that you honor His sovereignty?

Someone who had a very close encounter with Jesus wrote to me, "The closer you get to Jesus,
the more He demands that we honor His sovereignty." Can you imagine the opposite? Can you
imagine thinking that you can be closer to Jesus and just disregard His will and disregard His
sovereignty and disrespect who He is and His wisdom and His power? When you do that, you

start thinking more of yourself and your own plans and your own ideas and your own desires. Can you imagine that happening as you get closer to Jesus? That's not what happens. What happens is the closer you get, the more you realize what a sinner you are. All the great mystics of history wrote about that similarly. As they grew older, they didn't brag about how much they had progressed or how holy they had become. They didn't become experts in teaching other people to be like them. They took pains to make people realize that they were jars of clay. In the upside-down nature of the Kingdom, when we are weak we are strong. It's very, very simple.

PRESENCE PRAYER

O Lord, find me on my face today, drawing closer and closer to You.

BIBLE STUDY

The Scriptures reveal how God exercises His power. Beginning with Ephesians 1:11, embark on a study to find those places in Scripture that speak of God's Sovereignty. Once you have an adequate list, create a definition of God's sovereignty from a biblical perspective.

Day
5

HIS HOME IN YOUR HEART

Then Christ will make his home in your hearts as you trust in him. Your roots will grow down into God's love and keep you strong. And may you have the power to understand, as all God's people should, how wide, how long, how high, and how deep his love is. May you experience the love of Christ, though it is too great to understand fully. Then you will be made complete with all the fullness of life and power that comes from God.
—Ephesians 3:17-19 NLT

LIVING IN AND FROM HIS PRESENCE IS ABOUT TRYING TO COMPREHEND THE love He has for you. The more you trust Him, the more deeply in love you will become and the more you will understand His great love for you. Approaching Him through that love is how to live in the Presence and reach out to others from the Presence. It is how we allow Christ to make His home in our hearts.

For most of us, home is the center of our world. "There's no place like home!" according to Dorothy (*The Wizard of Oz*). At the end of her quest for home, Dorothy found a man behind a curtain, pretending to be great and powerful. When we seek Jesus with all our heart, we won't find what Dorothy found. When you seek God with all your heart, the One you will find is Jesus Christ, the One who tore the curtain in half! How marvelous is it that Jesus will make His home in your heart if you just ask Him? He is Immanuel, the good Shepherd, the Lamb of God. He is the anointed One, eternal, sent from God—the exact image of the invisible God. And He will come to dwell in your heart! It is too wonderful to fully comprehend. He will become the spiritual center of your life when you receive Him by faith.

BIBLE STUDY

Read Ephesians 3:14-21. In verse 19 Paul speaks of being filled to the measure of all the fullness of God. In order to allow God to fill you in this way, He must have access to your heart. Reflect on some of the things you think happen when you give God full access to your heart.

Notes

Session
4

ENCOUNTERING HIS PRESENCE

Heidi Baker

As God's co-workers we urge you not to receive God's grace in vain. For he says, "In the time of my favor I heard you, and in the day of salvation I helped you." I tell you, now is the time of God's favor, now is the day of salvation.
—2 Corinthians 6:1-2

SUMMARY

Did you know there are *kairos* moments when you can experience the Presence of God—life-shattering, life-transitioning moments? That's what we need! We need God to break in and change everything. We need to be in season with the Spirit in that place where God speaks to us like He spoke to Mary through the angel, saying, "You're going to carry a child." And Mary said, "I can't. I'm a virgin." The answer: "I can. I'm God." All you have to say is, "Yes, God, use me."

To encounter His Presence in this way is a lifestyle—a lifestyle of drawing away with God. It's not a stressed-out, "Oh, I hope God shows up!" kind of lifestyle. No, you *know* God will show up because you live with Him. You live in His Presence, and when you live in His Presence God takes your little bitty heart and He breaks it wide open—and you find yourself living in radical compassion. You put the clock, the watch, behind your back and you say, "Yes, Lord," and God does the miraculous! We're just all little tiny people on a little tiny planet, but when we learn to live in the Presence, to live in the embrace of God, everything changes. Absolutely everything changes.

INTERACTIVE QUESTIONS

1. The Bible speaks often of *kairos* time. Read Second Corinthians 6:1-2. As you reflect on this passage, ask yourself what it reveals to you about the meaning of *kairos* time.

_____

_____

_____

_____

_____

_____

2. What are your thoughts on taking up a lifestyle of desperation such as Heidi describes? How desperate do you want to be?

3. The issue of surrender is a difficult one for most people. What's getting in the way of your complete surrender to God? Find at least one person in the Bible who had difficulty surrendering to God and reflect on their story.

_____

_____

_____

_____

_____

_____

4. Reflect on the nature of miracles as found in the Gospel of Mark, and identify two or three types of miracles. How do you explain the relationship between miracles and faith?

_____

_____

_____

_____

_____

_____

_____

_____

5. Miracles that seem to us to be outside God's divine laws of nature, such as turning water into wine, may in fact be consistent with aspects of God's nature we are simply not familiar with. What are your thoughts on this statement?

_____

_____

_____

_____

_____

_____

_____

_____

_____

ACTIVATION EXERCISES

Group Activation

We encounter God's presence in the fullness of His time—in *kairos* moments. Take a few minutes to search the Scriptures for instances of God's *kairos* time. When everyone has at least a few scriptures, as a group, identify the meaning of *kairos* in each scripture. Mark 1:14-15 is an example of where the word *kairos* has a specific meaning. It speaks of a time that demands transformation.

Individual Activation

Search the Bible for instances of God's *kairos* time. Then spend time with the Lord, asking Him to show you how you might take what He teaches you about *kairos* time from Scripture and apply it to the season you are currently in as it relates to the culture around you.

Day
1

A LIFESTYLE OF LIVING IN HIS PRESENCE

I will remember the deeds of the Lord; yes, I will
remember your miracles of long ago.
—PSALM 77:11

THE OLD TESTAMENT IS FILLED WITH THE MIRACLES OF GOD—FROM CREATION to parting the sea to a talking donkey and many others. God is the God of miracles. Being present with Him is being in the Presence of miracles.

Do you want to say yes to living in His Presence, to living in the glory? To living in the favor where compassion rules your heart and miracles are commonplace? I'm not suggesting some one-time, "Oh, let's have a miracle rally, a miracle crusade! It will be great!" No. I'm challenging us to take up a lifestyle of desperation—being desperate for Jesus 24/7. The world is desperate! They're desperate for us—for you—to carry the glory of God to them. People are desperate for you to carry the power of the Almighty God to them. When you to step out in faith and touch others—everyone you come in contact with—with the love of God, you are living in His Presence. You're not afraid. You're living lean. You're living holy. You're living pure. You're in season, out of season, ready any time. You know Daddy's got your back, and Daddy knows your name. And when He calls, you come. He's a good Daddy, and every day He will call your name.

Like Moses who wanted the Lord's Presence always to go with him, this can be our conversation with God as well. We want to please Him, to learn from Him and find favor with Him. We want Him to remember our nation and its people, for we need Him—not politicians or celebrities—to lead us in all our endeavors. When we are sincere and obey His commands, His Presence will go with us and we will find rest and peace.

BIBLE STUDY

Reflect on Jeremiah 32:27: *"I am the Lord, the God of all mankind. Is anything too hard for me?"* then read First Kings 17, the story of the poor widow who was sustained by God through a famine. God took a jar of flour and a jug of oil and provided all she needed during her time of desperation. This poor woman wasn't anyone "special" in the eyes of the world, yet she was so very special in the heart of God, and so are you. Reflect on how God has provided for you.

Day
2

RADICAL LOVE,
RADICAL PRESENCE

Do not conform to the pattern of this world, but be transformed
by the renewing of your mind. Then you will be able to test and
approve what God's will is—his good, pleasing and perfect will.
—ROMANS 12:2

I KNOW WHEN I'M OUT OF THE PRESENCE BECAUSE I START TO FEEL THE STRESS. I look at the bank account and wonder how everything will work out. Stress! But when I'm in the Presence, I'm totally trusting in a completely trustworthy God. And everything is possible with Him. Rocks fall to the ground, machine guns break in half, God moves walls, creates food. When God puts His Spirit in you and you live in the Presence, then everybody will recognize it. They will see you sold out, radical, and wrecked for Jesus and will want what you have. Believe that God will crash in with His radical Presence when you say, "Yes!" And then watch out because He is a God of radical love. He won't come and leave you the same.

Get connected to the very One who is worthy—Jesus—so connected to Him that your life is not your own. Get to the place where there's so much "yes" in you that there isn't any room for "no." Become radically yielded and watch His Presence overtake everything.

PRESENCE PRAYER

*Come, sweet Jesus, be with us. If Your presence doesn't go with us, we're not going anywhere. Lord, we want a show and tell. We don't want to just hear about Your Presence, Lord. We want to be possessed by the One who is worthy—Jesus. We want to be undone. We want joy unspeakable and full of glory! We yield our hearts to You. God, we choose You. We want to be wrecked by You, undone by You, loved by You, God. We are listening for You, our Father, to call us by name. When we hear You call, we will answer, "**Yes, Lord, use me**."*

SCRIPTURE REFLECTION

Read Luke 6:48, then reflect on your foundation. How radical is your foundation? What is the correlation between foundation and the will of God?

Day 3

DEPENDENT ON MIRACLES

WE AT IRIS GLOBAL DEPEND ON MIRACLES FOR EVERYTHING—EVERY LITTLE detail. We depend on miracles for the love in our hearts, for our patience, for understanding, for our vision, for initiatives, for ideas, and for financial resources. And we have learned that God doesn't tell us too much in advance. He tells us what we need to know when we need to know it. You may have noticed that in your life as well. If He told us in advance, we wouldn't need His magnificent miracles because we would come up with our own six-month plan—and then think we didn't need Him for six months.

When we speak at conferences and other events, we do it not to get anything from the people. In fact, that's not what our ministry is at all. We are all about helping others through sharing the Word of God with them by ministering to their basic physical needs and to their spiritual needs in unison. We know that we are not really free in the love of Jesus until there are no ulterior motives. We're not trying to get affection or even friendship. We're not trying to get money, support, or admiration. We just offer the love of Christ, which sets us free—free to accept the miracles God sends our way.

All that being said, the simple fact of the matter is that most of our prayers for miracles don't get answered. Why not? God is not obligated to do anything we say or ask for. In fact, because God is perfect, we are not able to persuade Him to do something that isn't perfect. Unless your will coincides with His, unless it's perfect in His opinion, the answer will be no. God's agenda is different from ours. His agenda is to destroy everything in our hearts that doesn't come from the Holy Spirit—until we have no will of our own. None. Nobody wants to be a robot unless we get desperate enough.

Rolland and I have been in places and times when we are so desperate, so incredibly desperate; there are multiple crises and so many challenges; we are totally out of ideas and don't know where to turn or what to do; we have no concept of what step to take next. That's when I've been known to throw myself onto my bed and plead, "God, I would love to be on Your puppet strings. Move me, use me to accomplish *Your* will, not mine."

PRESENCE PRAYER

As the Spirit leads you, speak out your own prayer to God today to become a puppet on His strings, surrendering your will to God's will. If possible, record your prayer and then transcribe it so that you have it for future prayer times.

BIBLE STUDY

Go through the gospels and find those places where Jesus performed miracles, making note of His complete dependency on the Father at all times.

Day
4

LIVING WITH A FREE
AND HOLY HEART

WHAT HAPPENS WHEN GOD CHANGES YOUR HEART? I THINK THAT'S THE biggest miracle of all because there's no tougher challenge in all the world, no heavier burden you could ever have than to tell someone, "Be holy." God has to make you holy. Holy Spirit has to make you holy, and He's the only One who can do it. The question is, "What happens when He changes your heart?" When He changes your heart, you delight to do His will. His will becomes the greatest thing you could ever imagine doing—and when you're able to do it, you can't believe you get to do it!

There was a time when God told me to move to the slums of Hong Kong, or to give away huge amounts of money, or go to some impossible place or situation, or forgive an absolutely unforgivable person. I was utterly unable to do any of this outside of a changed heart. When you find yourself saying "yes" and "I can't believe I get to do this!" that's when you know you are set free. You're not contending with God. You're not trying to control Him and change His will. You're not trying to fight Him. You are delighting in surrendering completely, because you realize that your life doesn't belong to you anymore. It belongs to Him! You've been bought at a price, and your life is no longer yours.

Rolland was supposed to be dead seven years ago. Doctors gave him two weeks to live. He was declining over a two-year period. It was terrible. He was at the gates of hell for a long time, but every minute he lives and breathes now is God's. I love that God is in control. I love that He is the boss.

So how do we get the miracles that we need? Do Rolland and I equip ourselves a certain way? My answer is, "I have no idea other than to live in the Presence." That's what this interactive manual is all about—helping you understand about living in the Presence. I do not want to live outside His Presence. Not that we don't need miracles; we need them all the time more than we can even imagine. And God is gifting us with miracles every day in a million different ways. The miracle of a child's birth, sunshine, good health, a sense of humor and compassion, relationships, books, water, and on and on—each a miracle, gifts from God that can't be bought or measured in our finite minds.

SCRIPTURE REFLECTION

Read Psalm 51:10-12,17:

Create in me a pure heart, O God, and renew a steadfast spirit within me. Do not cast me from your presence or take your Holy Spirit from me. Restore to me the joy of your salvation and grant me a willing spirit, to sustain me. … My sacrifice, O God, is a broken spirit; a broken and contrite heart you, O God, will not despise (NIV).

Create a new, clean heart within me. Fill me with pure thoughts and holy desires, ready to please you. May you never reject me! May you never take from me your Scared Spirit! Let my passion for life be restored, tasting joy in every breakthrough you bring to me! Hold me close to you with a willing spirit that obeys whatever you say. …The fountain of your pleasure is found in the sacrifice of my shattered heart before you. You will not despise my tenderness as I humbly bow down at your feet! (TPT)

When you have had time to let these words of Scripture penetrate your heart, pray them aloud to God.

Day 5

ENCOUNTER HIM IN THE MIRACULOUS

He performs wonders that cannot be fathomed,
miracles that cannot be counted.
—JOB 5:9; 9:10

IT MAY BE AN EXCITING VENTURE TO KEEP A LITTLE NOTEBOOK IN YOUR POCKET or purse and write down every miracle you encounter in your daily life. God will surprise you!

The New Testament is chock-full of miracles. You'll find the miracles of Jesus in the gospels, and the miracles He did through His disciples in the early church, after His death, in the power of the Holy Spirit. Nothing has changed in that regard—Jesus is still performing miracles through His disciples today, in the power of Holy Spirit. They are happening all around us, all over the world. I love the story of the Samaritan woman at the well from John 4. This woman encountered the living God in a miraculous way. The Spirit revealed to her how *"true worshipers will worship the Father in the Spirit and in truth, for they are the kind of worshipers the Father seeks"* (John 4:23). To encounter His Presence in the miraculous is to worship Him. You can't help yourself! When His Presence shows up miraculously, worship just comes out of you because your heart was created by Him and for Him.

The Samaritan woman had a transformation encounter in the power of the Spirit that took her out of a broken lifestyle and into God's river of living water. She walked up to draw water from Jacob's well with an Old Covenant mindset and ended up receiving Living Water from the Source and went away with the New Covenant in her heart. How miraculous is that! God took a broken woman and healed her by the power of His Presence in Jesus and then sent her home to evangelize. Her whole village came to Christ, and it just spread from there. That's miraculous! God is "outside the box" with the miraculous. Nothing is safe! Every earthly paradigm is shattered to make way for Heaven's invasion!

PRESENCE PRAYER

Cry out to God now! Ask Him to take your little life and throw it into His river of Living Water until you drown there, dying to self and rising to new life in Jesus.

BIBLE STUDY

The Bible is full of epic miracles, beginning in the Old Testament. Do a study and find approximately a dozen miracles in the Bible, making note of how you encounter God in each of these miracles.

Notes

Session
5

CLINGING TO HIS PRESENCE IN CHALLENGES

Heidi Baker

SUMMARY

Living in God's Presence is all about being in His embrace. We want to live inside God's embrace, to feel His arms around us, His love surrounding us. When you are in God's embrace, you are where He is and He is where you are. My absolute favorite chapter on God's presence is Exodus 33. There are many beautiful aspects of His character we can learn from this chapter. Like Moses, we want God to be pleased with us so He will teach us His ways and His will for our lives. We want to feel favored by God—ultimately feeling His embrace and sensing Him saying, "Look at My team. Look at My family. I want to hug them. I want to go with them on their life journey and give them rest when they are weary." That's living in God's embrace! When we are in His embrace, life's challenges give way to His mighty Presence.

INTERACTIVE QUESTIONS

1. Heidi highlights three aspects of God's character from Exodus 33. What is your take-away from these passages?

   [Moses said,] "If you are pleased with me, teach me your ways so I may know you and continue to find favor with you...."

   The Lord replied, "My Presence will go with you, and I will give you rest."

   Then Moses said to him, "If your Presence does not go with us, do not send us up from here."

   ...And the Lord said, "I will cause all my goodness to pass in front of you, and I will proclaim my name, the Lord, in your presence" (Exodus 33:13-15,19).

2. Are you a Mary or a Martha? Are you living in the moment or constantly distracted? Explain.

3. How do you answer the question, "What distinguishes you from other people on the face of the earth?"

4. What does it mean to be a "hard sell" like Pharaoh?

5. Using examples from Scripture other than the prodigal son, how does Father God respond to wayward hearts?

_____

_____

_____

_____

_____

_____

_____

6. Search the New Testament and find at least two places where Jesus brings the spiritually dead to life. How did He accomplish this?

_____

_____

_____

_____

ACTIVATION EXERCISES

Read Exodus 33, looking for the beautiful aspects of God's character. When Moses petitions the Lord in prayer on behalf of the people of Israel, God responds graciously. Notice in verse 12 that Moses is not willing to settle for an angel to accompany them; he desires the very Presence of God, and God does not deny him.

Group Activation

Read Exodus 33, making note of the beautiful aspects of God's character found in this portion of Scripture. Share with others, with a focus on the desire of Moses for God's Presence.

Individual Activation

Read Exodus 33, making note of the beautiful aspects of God's character found in this chapter. Reflect on Moses' desire for the Presence of God versus an angel. Based on your knowledge of Scripture, did Moses set a precedent for the way in which we are to relate to God?

Day
1

LIVING IN THE MOMENT
WITH GOD

"Martha, Martha," the Lord answered, "you are worried and upset about
many things, but few things are needed—or indeed only one. Mary
has chosen what is better, and it will not be taken away from her."
—LUKE 10:41-42

MARY WAS LIVING IN THE MOMENT; MARTHA WAS DISTRACTED. LIKE MARY, allow yourself to become absorbed by God; connect with Him, and He will connect with you in an embrace of His Presence. An embrace by God means being where He is and God being where you are—in the moment, every moment. The result is always lovely.

Rolland and I live in Mozambique, a country in Southeast Africa. We've been here in the land of revival for twenty-two years. Together with our teams, we have led hundreds of thousands of people to the Lord over the years. One of the ways God reveals Himself to the people here is through His miracles. The blind see, the deaf hear, and the crippled walk. It's been an awesome experience and one we greatly cherish. However, life in Mozambique is full of challenges, large and small. If we don't stay moment by moment in God's Presence, those challenges can overwhelm us. I invite God into every moment because life is so much sweeter when He is present.

I recall one Saturday when God's Presence transformed a small inconvenience in my day. Saturday is our Sabbath day. I typically don't leave the house. Instead, I like to worship, get in the Word, listen to audio books, and just soak in God's Presence. It's my day alone with Papa God, and I eagerly look forward to it all week. On this particular Saturday I was enjoying time in His marvelous Presence when suddenly I remembered that I *had* to go to the bank. My tendency was to respond like "Martha"—to grumble about how my intimate time alone with God was going to be interrupted.

I drove to the bank, and on the way back to our base, the Village of Joy, my "Martha" mindset began to give way to a "Mary" mindset as I thought about the name of our base, "Village of Joy." What an awesome name; what an awesome place! God is always there and revival crashes in routinely. Hundreds of people receive the Lord and are baptized in the Holy Spirit at the base. Sometimes thousands at a time come under the weighty Presence of the Lord and fall to the floor where they remain, often for hours. Just thinking about it brought me into His glorious Presence right there in the car. My day alone with Him wasn't ruined. It just took place in a different way when I allowed His Presence to set my heart aright.

PRESENCE PRAYER

Gracious Father, crash in on me today with Your "Mary" mindset. I invite You into every aspect of my day—the large and the small. I want to live moment by moment with You in the embrace of Your Presence.

SCRIPTURE REFLECTION

Read and reflect on Proverbs 4:23: "*Keep your heart with all vigilance, for from it flow the springs of life*" (ESV). How is the placement of Heidi's heart a spring of life for her and others?

Day 2

FACING CHALLENGES WITH GOD'S PRESENCE

*Then Moses said to him, "If your Presence does not
go with us, do not send us up from here."*
—EXODUS 33:15

IF WE ARE THINKING WISELY LIKE MOSES, NO MOVE OR DECISION SHOULD BE made without the Presence of God with us. In verse 16, Moses asks God, *"How will anyone know that you are pleased with me and with your people unless you go with us? What else will distinguish me and your people from all the other people on the face of the earth?"* Excellent question! I love

God's answer. He says, *"I will do the very thing you have asked, because I am pleased with you and I know you by name"* (Exod. 33:17). God and Moses had a personal relationship. Relationship brought His Presence.

Challenges in Mozambique can happen quickly, like the riot that ensued one day right in front of the Village of Joy. It was the Saturday I was driving back from the bank, reflecting on God's amazing presence on the Village of Joy. As I drove up, I saw people beating each other. There were armed guards—police with machine guns. A group of youth called the Glory Boys were beating up some of the police officers. I saw some international people from our Harvest School walking toward the riot. Jumping out of the car, I started yelling to the Harvest School students, "Get out of the way! Go back!" As they turned and went in the other direction, I started walking toward the gunfire because that's what mamas do. Youths were attacking the police and the police were shooting. I waded into the crowd, yelling, "Stop it! Stop it! No shooting here on this base." One police officer was bloody and a couple of the street kids were bloody. It was not a peaceful scene. The police took away one of the boys, and then the rioting started again. People gathered around my car shouting, "Go get that guy out of jail! You better go get him out!"

"Jesus, Jesus, what do I do?" I prayed. I decided to drive to the police station. Inside, I found one of the youth who had attacked the police. "We're going to beat him for a week and teach him a lesson," one of the police was saying. No sooner were the words out of his mouth than the policemen from the riot walked in. They were shaking. "I don't understand. I don't understand," one of them said. "My machine gun broke in two."

BIBLE STUDY

Much of the church thinks that God does not perform miracles today. Heidi's experience, and that of many others, constantly refutes that thinking. Read Daniel 6:1-23, reflecting on this incredible miracle story of rescue. What was it about Daniel in this story that brought God's favor, and how does it tie in to today's message?

Day
3

THE GOODNESS OF GOD

Now the Lord said to Moses, "Go in to Pharaoh...that I may show these signs
of Mine before him, and that you may tell in the hearing of your son...My signs
which I have done among them, that you may know that I am the Lord."
—Exodus 10:1-2 NKJV

THE PRESENCE OF GOD IS NOT ONLY FOUND IN A BEAUTIFUL CHURCH, FILLED with well-dressed people, with great spiritual music playing. The Presence of God is also walking beside rioters and peacekeepers and innocent bystanders. He is embracing the down and out, the persecuted, the believers trying to do right by Him. Hallelujah! Sometimes, the best time to find the manifest Presence of God is in the middle of a riot when the God of the universe takes an AK-47 and snaps it in half! That's my God! I need Him! I need His Presence, always and everywhere. You do too.

God did a miracle that day at the gate to the Village of Joy. His manifest Presence is for every single moment of our lives—the hard moments, the good moments—all of them. It's not just once a week when you're in a room with a whole lot of believers or when you are at home celebrating a glorious, quiet Sabbath on your knees. No, God's Presence is available for every moment of every day. God will crash in whenever you call on Him. He'll come right in the middle of machine gun fire and break a machine gun in half!

Most people learn easily from show and tell. Not so Pharaoh who heard God's intentions and saw His mighty power. God had to show Pharaoh plague after plague before he finally understood that God was serious. Are you a "hard sell," or is your heart softened by the goodness of the Lord?

BIBLE STUDY

Read the story of Rahab found in Joshua 2:1-6 and 6:17, reflecting on how the hunger in her heart to know God not only rescued her (saved her life and the life of her family), it also redeemed her. Note other stories in the Bible, in both the Old and New Testaments, where God rescues and redeems. How has He rescued and redeemed you?

Day
4

A FATHER'S EMBRACE

But his father said to the servants, "Quick! Bring the finest robe in
the house and put it on him. Get a ring for his finger and sandals for
his feet. And kill the calf we have been fattening. We must celebrate
with a feast, for this son of mine was dead and has now returned
to life. He was lost, but now he is found." So the party began.
—LUKE 15:22-24 NLT

THE STORY OF THE PRODIGAL SON ENDS WITH A WELCOME-HOME EMBRACE. From a wayward son who wastes his inheritance to being welcomed home by his father, we can identify with this "I-want-it-my-way" son. Too often we ask for things we are not ready to have—not prepared to handle correctly. When we are out of God's will and destiny, we invite disaster, realizing too late that God's way is the best way. The father welcomed his son home *"filled with love and compassion,"* running to him with open arms and enveloping him with a warm embrace. This is the same scene played over and over throughout the ages when any of God's children strike out on their own only to realize their error and return home, repentant. God's embrace is as real and tangible as the father's in this story that Jesus told those many years ago. When we come to our senses, as did the son, we must run back to the Father's Presence and stay there, asking for forgiveness, until we feel His warm embrace. Our contrite hearts are what He sees first as we are running toward Him. Does He ever tire of our waywardness? Surely, yes, but He never turns us away.

Don't expect a faux hug and air kisses when you seek God's Presence. Nothing short of a hearty bear hug and kisses firmly planted on each cheek and perhaps your forehead should be expected from your Creator God, the Lover of your soul. Just as a mother and a father of a newborn gaze with loving eyes at their little one, imagining the future—so does the Father look at you. As with the Prodigal Son, the Lord had already put in place His mercy and grace for His wayward children.

BIBLE REFLECTION

"My wayward children," says the Lord, *"come back to me, and I will heal your wayward hearts."* *"Yes, we're coming,"* the people reply, *"for you are the Lord our God"* (Jeremiah 3:22 NLT).

At this point in your life, are you feeling less or more wayward when it comes to heart issues?

Day 5

BREATHE DEEPLY OF HIS PRESENCE

"We must celebrate with a feast, for this son of mine was dead and has now returned to life. He was lost, but now he is found." So the party began.
—LUKE 15:23-24 NLT

FEELING LIFELESS IS MORE AND MORE COMMON TODAY, EVEN IN THIS AGE OF instant communication and information. True life and living comes only through the Living Word—Jesus Christ. Embracing the truths in the Bible brings breaths of fresh air. Jesus is inviting you to breathe deeply and live!

Paul, in his letter to the Corinthians, says that although we live here in our earthly bodies, the Lord's spiritual Presence is with us daily as we live by faith. We are God's treasures in jars of clay, showing His all-surpassing power.

> *We are hard pressed on every side, but not crushed; perplexed, but not in despair; persecuted, but not abandoned; struck down, but not destroyed. We always carry around in our body the death of Jesus, so that the life of Jesus may also be revealed in our body. For we who are alive are always being given over to death for Jesus' sake, so that his life may also be revealed in our mortal body. So then, death is at work in us, but life is at work in you* (2 Corinthians 4:8-12).

Living from the Presence is not about trying to figure out a myriad of different priorities and going in all directions. It is not about having a slew of ambitions and exploring all the possibilities or experiencing every kind of vision and responding to a variety of callings. You don't have to know any of that except and unless and as He reveals these things to you. Believe me, if you love Jesus He's going to use you. He will use you however He needs you, for the purpose you were given before you were born. The key is to be completely pliable, completely obedient, completely in love. When you are really in love with somebody, you're not arguing with that person all the time. You're not contending all the time. You're not begging all the time. You are satisfied with the person you love and allow yourself to be used. The key is to breathe deeply of His Presence, then die to self so that He can raise you to new spiritual life. Alive in His Presence, you will find fullness of joy!

PRESENCE PRAYER

Sweet Jesus, I breathe You in. Come now and fill all of me with Your life-giving Presence. Put me on Your potter's wheel; mold me, make me new, bend me, shape me until I look like You. I want to taste Your joy and Your peace. I want to feel Your embrace and live in Your Presence. I need You in the challenges and the triumphs. May You always find me a willing and obedient lover! Amen.

Notes

Session
6

PRACTICAL KEYS TO EXPERIENCING HIS PRESENCE

Heidi Baker

SUMMARY

What does the Presence look like? For me, one day the Presence looked like a broken machine gun. Other days it looks like the glory cloud. Glory looks like something; Presence looks like something. In Exodus 33, the Presence looks like a combination of God's Word, a promise, an angel, power to destroy the enemy, prosperity. The Lord told Moses to leave, to get up and get out of that place and go to his place of promise. *"Leave this place, you and the people you brought up out of Egypt, and go up to a land I promised on oath"* (Exod. 33:1).

For me, that land God promised me on oath is Mozambique. Maybe my twenty-two years there should have been easy. Maybe the Presence of God just wafts in at all times in such a way that I never feel the stress. Well, that hasn't been the case—but no matter the stress, His peace is so deep and so connected to Him that each challenge is defeated even before I face it. Moses has a promise from God. If you want to know about the Presence, you have to know about your promise. When I knew I had to face the angry crowd and the machine guns, there was something inside supporting me. I had no earthly weapon. The weapon I walked in with was our big God. I knew His Presence would manifest in the perfect way for the situation because He promised me. When you live in His Presence, promises come to pass. God never retracts His promises. All you need to do is accept the promises in faith.

INTERACTIVE QUESTIONS

1. What do you think about living in God's Presence to such a great extent that His power is present to make the enemy tremble? What is Heidi talking about with this statement?

_____

_____

_____

_____

2. How would you explain to someone what it means to "get out there in the Presence of Jesus"?

_____

_____

_____

_____

_____

_____

_____

_____

3. Heidi talks about "unpacking God" so that He can overshadow you with His Presence. What is she talking about? As you reflect on this question, think about Mary, the mother of Jesus. She had obviously "unpacked" God because of the way in which she responded when His Presence overshadowed her. What do the ways in which you have responded to God indicate about how you unpack your heavenly Father?

_____

_____

_____

_____

_____

_____

_____

_____

4. When Heidi talks about "living lean" in the Presence of God, she's not talking about losing weight, although she could be. What does it mean to "live lean"?

_____

_____

_____

_____

_____

_____

_____

_____

_____

5. When God uses the term "stiff-necked," it's not meant to be endearing. What implications does the term "stiff-necked" as God uses it in Scripture have for you?

_____

_____

_____

_____

_____

_____

_____

_____

6. In Romans, Paul talks about exchanging the glory of immortal God for things of no value. What does it mean to exchange the glory of God? Has any of this kind of exchange taken place in your life?

_____

_____

_____

_____

_____

_____

_____

_____

7. What does promise have to do with experiencing His Presence?

_____

_____

_____

_____

_____

_____

_____

_____

_____

_____

ACTIVATION EXERCISES

Group Activation

As a way of better understanding practical keys to experiencing God's Presence, reflect silently on those times when you have experienced God's Presence because of His promises. Share your experiences.

Individual Activation

As a way of better understanding practical keys to experiencing God's Presence, reflect on those times when you have experienced God's Presence because of His promises. Make note of those instances and hold them in your heart for those times in the future when you'll need to remember His promises when in need of His Presence.

Day
1

BE STRONG AND COURAGEOUS

Be strong and courageous. Do not be afraid or terrified because of them, for the Lord your God goes with you; he will never leave you nor forsake you.
—DEUTERONOMY 31:6

THE FIRST TIME I SAW ANGELS I WAS TOTALLY UNDONE. I WILL NEVER FORGET IT as long as I live. I was a student at Vanguard University and the host of a conference. The speaker that day was so annoying to me. I thought he was arrogant. At one point he said that God told him He was going to "give him a city." That really pushed me over the edge. I thought, *Oh, please; God doesn't give people cities. What do you mean God's giving you a city?* I'm arguing with this guy in my head, thinking how I don't want to take him to lunch, when whoosh! An angel showed up to the right of the man. Then, whoosh, another one appeared to his left. I was seeing them outside of my own eyes. And standing right behind the man was Jesus! Jesus pointed right at me and said, "Listen to him. He's telling the truth!"

I literally fell out of my chair, hit the deck and started sobbing. When the meeting was over, I crawled to the back to the prayer room and lifted my hands and worshiped for three and a half hours. "Lord," I said, "if You're giving someone a city, then I want a nation." That's what I said to God that day. His manifest presence left me utterly undone. Presence changes everything.

God said to Moses, *"I will send an angel before you and drive out the Canaanites, Amorites, Hittites, Perizzites, Hivites and Jebusites"* (Exod 33:2)—all the demonic tribes would be cast out so the people of God would have a clear path to the Promised Land. Moses and the Israelites had to be strong and courageous to walk that path. God wants you to live in the Presence because there you have power that causes the enemy to tremble. God doesn't intend for you to live life afraid. *He wants you to be strong and courageous in His Presence.* When demons flee, you know you're in the Presence!

SCRIPTURE REFLECTION

In Exodus 33, God tells Moses He may destroy the people, yet a few books of the Bible later He tells Moses the He would never leave them or forsake the people. How patient, tolerant, merciful, and gracious is our God! How has God displayed these aspects of His character in your life?

Day
2

BELIEVE IN HIM

The whole land of Canaan, where you now reside as a
foreigner, I will give as an everlasting possession to you and
your descendants after you; and I will be their God.
—GENESIS 17:8

TO LIVE FROM HIS PRESENCE MEANS THAT WE BELIEVE GOD IS WHO HE SAYS HE is. When you get out there "in the name of Jesus," you will find yourself in plenty of situations that require you to believe in Him. We had lived in the south of Mozambique for eight years and were totally excited about going north to reach the lost, the hidden people groups, the dying, and the desperate. We were eager to see God crash in and save lives. In our eagerness, we decided it would be good to bring in a super awesome anointed preacher, someone who carried the fire of God. We found our guy and flew him in. The plan was to go to an unreached people group of another faith, set up our gear and watch the fire fall. We forgot that the devil might have other plans.

The day of the conference, we set up our sound system in front of a crowd of about a thousand people. The preacher tried to preach, but the sound system wouldn't work properly. It just screeched and screeched. The people had arrived with rocks in their hands, and I don't mean little rocks. They were carrying big rocks and were about to throw them at us. This famous preacher looked at me with wide eyes and said, "I thought we were in revival here."

I said, "Not yet, but we will be." I was thinking, "You carry fire! Bring the fire!" It was a disaster. I asked Rolland if he wanted to preach, but he said no; he just wanted to leave. "God, what do I do?" I said. "I love Your manifest Presence, but I'm not feeling any right now. Where are You? Help us! I have a promise from You that says, 'Go get the lost, make them a Bride.' Where is Your Presence?"

Then I heard the Lord as clearly as could be say, "Have an altar call."

"Seriously, God?" I said. "What kind of altar call?"

"Call all the demonized," He replied.

I looked out at the crowd and said loudly in their language, "Would any of you like to see the power of God? Would you like to see the Presence of God come here? If any of you have demons living inside you and you can't sleep and they hurt you and you're sure you're possessed—come up here to the altar call!"

The people were staring at me. Then some of the demons started manifesting, making growling sounds. About thirty-six people were possessed. One man's tongue rolled out and hit his chest. I didn't like what was happening. I didn't feel His Presence. Somebody else hit the cement and started slithering like a snake. Oh, God! Rolland and the famous preacher stopped praying and opened their eyes. I said, "God, what do I do now? What do I do now?"

He said, "Get rid of *them*."

I'd never done that before, but I said loudly, "In the name of Jesus Christ, get out!" And all the demons left, just like that! It was awesome. We didn't touch any of the people. The Presence was present. The people fell down and were stuck to the broken cement floor. They couldn't move their fingers. They couldn't move their toes. Their long tongues went right back into their mouths. Their eyes looked normal. Jesus Himself showed up and all the demons fled.

I wasn't sure what to do next, so I went out into the crowd, who had dropped their rocks in the Presence. I just went from one to the next, offering salvation through Jesus Christ. One by one by one they accepted Jesus as their Lord and Savior. When I reached the middle of the crowd, I said to one of the men, "Do you want to meet Jesus?" As the man stood up, a demon began to manifest again, growling at me. I said, "You are at the end of your possession of this man; *get out of him!*" and the demon left. When you get out there for Jesus you need to believe that He is going to show up, and He will!

BIBLE STUDY

Read the story of Moses and the Israelites. God promised the Promised Land to Abraham and then to Moses and to all their descendants. From the beginning, God wanted all humankind to enjoy His creation—starting out with the Garden of Eden where all that was needed was provided. What are God's promises for you today?

Day 3

LIVE OUTSIDE THE BOX WITH GOD

"For my thoughts are not your thoughts, neither are your ways my ways," declares the Lord.
—ISAIAH 55:8

IT IS SO EASY TO STUFF GOD INTO BOXES THAT CONFORM TO EVERYDAY circumstances. How many times have you had to unpack Him so He can overshadow you with His presence? Think about Noah. Now there was a man who embraced what it means to live outside the box with God. Up to the time of Noah, biblical scholars find no evidence that the earth had ever experienced rain. Yet here was a man of great faith (see Heb. 11:7) who took seriously the warnings from God of things not yet seen. On faith, he built an impossibly large ark in a dry, landlocked place in anticipation of a great flood that seemed improbable. Like the others mentioned in the Faith Hall of Fame in Hebrews 11, Noah was willing to live outside the box with God because he knew the Presence.

Living from the Presence brings life. Sometimes when we hear about the Presence, we automatically put God into a box that limits what we think He can and cannot do. The Presence doesn't look like God in a box. It looks like a man building a huge boat in anticipation of a flood that is going to wipe out the entire population of the world. The Presence looks like a man who led his people across an ocean that parted in front of them, into the wilderness where no earthly provision could sustain them, and then into the Promised Land. It's giving an altar call to an angry crowd of a thousand people of another faith with rocks in their hands and then watching demons flee in the Presence of Jesus. The Presence of God changes everything. Living outside the box in the Presence of God is being with Jesus Himself; it's being possessed by Holy Spirit. It's putting aside your thoughts to embrace the ways of God by faith.

BIBLE STUDY

Read Hebrews 11 in its entirety, noticing how all of the people highlighted did not receive what had been promised, yet God had something better for them. What was that something better? What has God had for you when you did not receive what you wanted or expected from Him?

Day
4

BE A YIELDED LOVER

*O Jerusalem, Jerusalem, the city that kills the prophets and stones God's
messengers! How often I have wanted to gather your children together as
a hen protects her chicks beneath her wings, but you wouldn't let me.*
—MATTHEW 23:37 NLT

DO YOU MOURN MORE FREQUENTLY FOR LOST PROSPERITY THAN YOU DO FOR
the lost people of the world?

The western world loves Exodus 33:3 where is says, *"Go up to the land flowing with milk and honey."* This speaks of prosperity and we love prosperity! Many think if they have prosperity, they have the Presence. The Presence doesn't look like prosperity; they don't necessarily go together. They can, but not always. God said He wasn't going along with Moses and the people into the land of plenty because they were a stiff-necked people, which might cause Him to destroy them along the way! *"When the people heard these distressing words, they began to mourn"* (Exod. 33:4). Have you mourned before the Lord and perhaps said, "God, I don't care. I've had promises. I've had power over the enemy. I've healed the sick in Jesus' name. I have all the money I need." And then He says in return, "I'm not going with you. You're not going to feel My Presence, know My Presence, or live in My Presence because you're stiff-necked."

Stiff-necked means we are not pliable in the Lord's hands. He wants to take us and make us pliable. He wants our necks to bend. He wants us to be yielded to Him—yielded lovers in His Presence. We need to stop being stiff-necked, stop living on a diet of fluff and puff that has no spiritual value. God wants us to yield to Him so He can strip away the fluff and the puff. If you're going to live in the Presence, you need to live lean. You need to get rid of everything that doesn't bring God glory. Some people ask, "Well, does that mean giving up material possessions?" I don't know. Does that mean your job, your profession? I don't know. Only you and Holy Spirit know what is holding you back from living fully in the Presence.

Holy Spirit tells you to live lean, listen for His voice. If you want to live in the Presence, living lean is when your mind is not being controlled by anything else, when your heart is not being controlled by anything else, but where all that is within you is focused on the holy face of Jesus.

BIBLE STUDY

Read Exodus 33:5-7:

> *"Now **take off your ornaments** and I will decide what to do with you." So **the Israelites stripped off their ornaments** at Mount Horeb. Now Moses used to take a tent and pitch it outside the camp some distance away, calling it the "tent of meeting." **Anyone inquiring of the Lord would go to the tent of meeting** outside the camp.*

Moses and the people stripped off their "ornaments" (distractions) at Mount Horeb and Moses pitched a tent outside the camp, pursuing the Presence. How much are you pressing into the Presence of God daily? What do you need to "put off" in order to come fully before God? Do you hunger for His Presence more than anything else?

Don't be afraid to be a yielded lover who does things outside the box. Your experience may be totally out of this world when you do!

Day 5

CAST OFF IDOLATRY

[The Lord said through Ezekiel,] *"You took the very jewels and gold and silver ornaments I had given you and made statues of men and worshiped them. This is adultery against me!"*
—EZEKIEL 16:17 NLT

USING "ORNAMENTS" FOR HIS GLORY IS THE ONLY JUSTIFICATION FOR ALL THE many things accumulated in our current western world of materialism. When you read the word *materialism*, did any "things" come to mind that you could do without, stuff that is distracting you from His Kingdom? We just addressed the issue of possessions in Day 4 of this session. Now

I want you to focus in on what it means to cast off idolatry, because idolatry comes in many forms besides possessions.

In Romans 1:21-25, Paul gives us the origin of idolatry:

For although they knew God, they neither glorified him as God nor gave thanks to him, but their thinking became futile and their foolish hearts were darkened. Although they claimed to be wise, they became fools and exchanged the glory of the immortal God for images made to look like a mortal human being and birds and animals and reptiles. Therefore God gave them over in the sinful desires of their hearts to sexual impurity for the degrading of their bodies with one another. They exchanged the truth about God for a lie, and worshiped and served created things rather than the Creator—who is forever praised.

This is a very harsh passage to read. God is reacting to what is contrary to and opposes His holy name. These people are worshiping graven images and the result is separation from God. I doubt that any of you reading this are worshiping graven images, but if you are, stop! My point in using this passage of Scripture is to take us to the biblical consequences of idolatry—separation from God. Any form of idolatry will separate you from God. Work can become an idol, knowledge, people, our ego—all of these idols can separate us from God. Deuteronomy 6:5 says, "*Love the Lord your God with all your heart and with all your soul and with all your strength.*" *Everything* within you is created to love God. When you operate outside your created purpose, you step away from God. You cannot live an adulterous life and experience His Presence.

FOCUS

Invite the Presence of God and ask Him to show you any area of your life that is separating you from Him. As He identifies areas of your life that need attention, write them down. When you are satisfied you have heard fully from God, go to Psalm 78 and make note of all the ways in which you can counter any tendencies to idolatry in your life. Some examples are to reverence God and meditate on His Word and His works. Keep both lists handy and refer to them often, because the tendency to idolatry is not overcome once, never to return. Idolatry can and will creep back into our lives and must be constantly identified and dealt with in order to live from a place of God's Presence.

PRESENCE PRAYER

Take time now to write your own prayer here. Let it flow from your heart straight to God's heart. Then keep your prayer on hand for the next time idolatry tries to creep back into your life and separate you from God.

Therefore confess your sins to each other and pray for each other so that you may be healed. The prayer of a righteous person is powerful and effective (James 5:16).

Notes

Session

7

YOUR IDENTITY IN HIS PRESENCE

Heidi Baker

SUMMARY

During this time of listening and watching and showing and telling, I believe that God is creating a holy hunger to not just *experience* His Presence, but to *live* in His manifest Presence; and not just to *live* in His manifest Presence, but to *carry* His manifest Presence, which is compassion and mercy and glory and kindness and meekness. We are to carry it into our homes, into our schools and the workplace, into the malls, the streets, the famine zones, and out among the unreached people groups of the world.

Jesus is the point of our existence. *"She will give birth to a son, and you are to give him the name Jesus, because he will save his people from their sins"* (Matt. 1:21). Before He was born, Jesus' purpose was to save us from ourselves—our sinful nature. Without Jesus we are lost, unable to be reunited with the heavenly Father. With Him we have purpose—His purpose. In Him we find identity—knowing who we are in Christ. There are many benefits of being saved. One of the most important is being connected to Jesus in our everyday lives. Jesus is the basis for the Kingdom-effect on earth.

Jesus was humble, always pointing to His heavenly Father, teaching people how to get closer to the Lord so they could live the abundant life promised to them. When asked by an expert in the law which of the commandments was the greatest, *"Jesus replied: 'Love the Lord your God with all your heart and with all your soul and with all your mind'"* (Matt. 22:37). What does it mean to love the Lord your God with all your heart and mind and soul and strength? Think about that. Is it possible for us to love with *all* of our heart, soul, and mind? Probably not. We need Holy Spirit to help us understand what our spirits are capable of. Holy Spirit will do that for you. All you have to do is ask.

INTERACTIVE QUESTIONS

1. The compassion of God in Jesus is displayed throughout the gospels. Find some examples of God's compassion in Scripture, in either the New or Old Testament. Then, identify examples of God's compassion in your life.

2. How can you stand beside Jesus in intercession to help build His church? Where in Scripture do we find the importance of intercession?

3. What does it mean to be "washed clean" so that others can see Jesus through us?

_____

_____

_____

_____

_____

_____

_____

_____

4. Heidi talks about becoming "humbly strong" like the humble Bridegroom. Identify some of the ways in which Jesus demonstrates humility for us in the Scriptures. How have you demonstrated His humility in your own environment?

_____

_____

_____

_____

_____

_____

_____

_____

_____

5. Heidi says that the only way we can live in the Presence is if we realize and recognize the love of the Father for His Son. How has God demonstrated this love? How do you think He wants you to demonstrate it?

_____

_____

_____

_____

_____

_____

_____

_____

ACTIVATION EXERCISES

Compassion is a very significant aspect of Jesus' character. And as Jesus is an exact representation of the Father, then it is also a significant aspect of God's character.

Group Activation

Reflect on God's compassion in your own life, thinking about how God's compassion toward you has made you more compassionate. Share as you feel led.

Individual Activation

Reflect on God's compassion in your life. How has God's compassion toward you made you more compassionate?

Day
1

MORE OF YOU, JESUS

And when Jesus went out He saw a great multitude; and He was moved with compassion for them, and healed their sick.
—MATTHEW 14:14 NKJV

JESUS WAS MOVED WITH COMPASSION FOR THE PEOPLE. HOW OFTEN ARE YOU moved with compassion?

Compassion is part of the character of Jesus, an attribute of who He is. Jesus is the manifestation of God to us as a perfect human companion, full of compassion. He is the One who died for us. Now that's compassion! That's why I go to Him—why you should go to Him. He has become to us everything. He has become to us our sanctification, our power, our glory, our initiative, our joy, our highest goal. Jesus is how God wants to be known. Otherwise He's just an invisible, infinite spirit like Muslims and others believe. What does it mean to want more of Jesus? It starts with hunger—spiritual hunger. You're not really hungry for Jesus until you're not satisfied with the way things are now. You can't make anybody hungry if they think they have already arrived and they are right where they should be and they are totally happy inside and everything's fine and there's nothing to ask for. Hunger springs from need. When you're dissatisfied, you are in need.

Those who came to Jesus for miracles were in need and He responded—with compassion. The Bible says Jesus healed out of compassion. *"When Jesus landed and saw a large crowd, he had compassion on them and healed their sick"* (Matt. 14:14). So how do we receive the compassion of Jesus in our hearts and why should we want it? To begin with, compassion is a true mark of Christian character. From Exodus through the Psalms and the prophets and into the gospels and the epistles, Scripture tells again and again that compassion is to mark the life of the believer. How hungry are you to bear the mark of Jesus—the compassion of Jesus in your life?

BIBLE REFLECTION

Read and reflect on Isaiah 30:18:

Yet the Lord longs to be gracious to you; therefore he will rise up to show you compassion. For the Lord is a God of justice. Blessed are all who wait for him!

What an amazing heavenly Father we have—He longs to be gracious to us and He will actually *rise up* and show us compassion. Explain the connection between compassion and justice.

Day 2

OUR GREAT INTERCESSOR

Therefore He is also able to save to the uttermost those who come to God through Him, since He always lives to make intercession for them.
—HEBREWS 7:25 NKJV

JESUS PRAYS FOR YOU DIRECTLY TO GOD THE FATHER. HE STANDS BETWEEN YOU and God, praying on your behalf. He loves you so much that He knows better than you what you need from your heavenly Father. Our salvation was secured by Jesus on the cross, yet we still have needs. That is why Jesus is our great intercessor. His care and loving-kindness toward us doesn't end; it's forever. It's ongoing. He sits at the right hand of the Father interceding for *us*. He is the

Good Shepherd, always caring for His sheep. He is the *one* mediator between God and man (see 1 Tim. 2:5).

Jesus is our great High Priest, and we are part of His priesthood of believers. In fact, we're a royal priesthood. *"But you are a chosen people, a royal priesthood, a holy nation, God's special possession, that you may declare the praises of him who called you out of darkness into his wonderful light"* (1 Pet. 2:9). As royal priests we have free access to His Presence. We are called to stand beside Him and help build His church. With Jesus we can come boldly before the throne of God and make our requests. We can enter the holy place with confidence because of Jesus. Our access as intercessors is a tremendous privilege! It is part of our inheritance and our identity.

SCRIPTURE REFLECTION

Read First Peter 2:. What positive applications can you find in this passage for the priesthood of believers?

Day
3

SERVANTHOOD

*Now before the Feast of the Passover, when Jesus knew that His hour had come that He should depart from this world to the Father, having loved His own who were in the world, **He loved them to the end.** ...He poured water into a basin and began to wash the disciples' feet, and to wipe them with the towel with which He was girded. Then He came to Simon Peter. And Peter said to Him, "Lord, are You washing my feet?" Jesus answered and said to him, "What I am doing you do not understand now, but you will know after this." Peter said to Him, "You shall never wash my feet!" Jesus answered him, "If I do not wash you, you have no part with Me." Simon Peter said to Him, "Lord, not my feet only, but also my hands and my head!"*
—John 13:1,5-9 NKJV

JESUS' DEVOTION

Ever overzealous, Peter couldn't believe that Jesus, the Son of God, was going to wash his feet. Peter vehemently refused to allow Jesus to do a servant's chore. He was devoted to the Savior and didn't want Jesus to lower Himself. When Jesus explained to Peter that it was an act He had to perform in accordance with His purpose on earth, then Peter wanted *more of Jesus*—he wanted Jesus to wash his feet and hands and head!

Do we want more of Jesus? Do you yearn for Him to wash you from the inside out? The more we know of Him, the more we should want of Him. We should be charter members of His fan club—willing to travel with Him, support His causes, hold Him up for others to see and love. When people see us, they should see Jesus living through us.

SCRIPTURE REFLECTION

Read Psalm 51:7-12:

Cleanse me with hyssop, and I will be clean; wash me, and I will be whiter than snow. Let me hear joy and gladness; let the bones you have crushed rejoice. Hide your face from my sins and blot out all my iniquity. Create in me a pure heart, O God, and renew a steadfast spirit within me. Do not cast me from your presence or take your Holy Spirit from me. Restore to me the joy of your salvation and grant me a willing spirit, to sustain me.

In Hebrew culture, hyssop was a plant used to sprinkle blood on a healed leper to ceremonially cleanse him for the worship of God. How does the sprinkled blood of Jesus "speak a better word"?

Day
4

THE HUMBLE BRIDEGROOM

He poured water into a basin and began to wash the
disciples' feet and to wipe them with the towel.
—John 13:5 ESV

HOW COULD YOU NOT WANT MORE OF JESUS WHEN YOU KNOW HE IS WILLING
to wash your feet because He loves you so much? Not only was He willing to wash His disciples'
feet, He was willing to shed His blood for you. With more of Him, you can change the world!

The Holy Spirit gives and builds the relationship we have with Jesus. Jesus is how God wants to be known and loved. He is the Bridegroom. We fall in love. We leave our parents to get married. Jesus is the Bridegroom of the Church, residing spiritually and deeply in our hearts where we most, most need Him. Paul says, "I have suffered the loss of all things for the surpassing value of knowing Christ Jesus my Lord." In Jesus we find the Father. In Jesus we have the presence and power of the Holy Spirit—and if we take our eyes off Jesus, we lose everything. That's why Paul made it so clear when he wrote, *"For I resolved to know nothing while I was with you except Jesus Christ and him crucified"* (1 Cor. 2:2).

We know that the only way forward anywhere in ministry is to be humble. That's the first step if you want to step out and make a difference. But don't try and make yourself humble. A humble spirit grows the closer you get to Jesus. His Spirit rubs off on you and you become humbly strong. Being humble doesn't mean you allow people to unduly influence you. You must stay strong in your faith, yet humble in your attitude toward people. When you want more of Jesus, He will infuse you with His Spirit, which will transform you in the best ways possible. Remember, He uses anyone open to doing His will. More, more of Jesus—we can never have enough of Him until He returns for us or God takes us home to Heaven.

> *Then the sign of the Son of Man will appear in heaven, and then all the tribes of the earth will mourn, and they will see the Son of Man coming on the clouds of heaven with power and great glory. And He will send His angels with a great sound of a trumpet, and they will gather together His elect from the four winds, from one end of heaven to the other. …But of that day and hour no one knows, not even the angels of heaven, but My Father only* (Matthew 24:30-31,36 NKJV).

SCRIPTURE REFLECTION

Read the story of the wedding at Cana in John 2:1-12. Notice how Jesus is not eager to reveal who He is. His mother urges Him to show Himself because she knows His identity. In verse three she tries to reason with Him by telling Jesus that the "bride" has no wine. Jesus is the Bridegroom, the New Wine. Jesus' response to His mother sounds a bit harsh in some translations. He basically says, "What's it to you, Mom?" What He is saying is that once His identity is revealed, everything will change. Boy, did everything change, for all eternity! How have you been changed by the new wine of the humble Bridegroom?

Day 5

LOVING LIKE JESUS

And walk in the way of love, just as Christ loved us and gave himself up for us as a fragrant offering and sacrifice to God.
—EPHESIANS 5:2

THE ONLY WAY YOU CAN LIVE IN THE PRESENCE IS IF YOU REALIZE AND recognize the love of the Father for His Son. Like God, you need to be deeply, deeply in love with Jesus. You know that if it's just you and Jesus—your family has given up on you, you've had failures, people have written you off, and you have nothing for anybody—you will have more than enough. If life comes down to just you and Jesus, rejoice. You don't have to compete anymore. You don't have to expand your mailing list. You don't have to get more support. You don't have to try to be more influential. You don't have to get another promotion. You don't need a platform. You don't need to get somewhere. You just need to be in love with your one and only Lover! You don't have to strive. You don't have to compete.

I don't have a technique for imparting love for Jesus. Lots of people e-mail me and say, "Yeah, that all sounds good, but how do I do that?" The answer is, "I don't know." All I do know is that we need to come to Jesus empty-handed, not claiming to have it figured out or know how to get Him to do it for you—we must be contrite, broken. If you know anything about Iris Global, you know that we're literally compelled by the love of God in Jesus. Love is central to who we are because it is central to who Jesus is. Jesus is God's love, a love big enough to touch any life.

One day I saw an old mama just rocking out in the sun. Mozambique is so hot nobody sits in the sun. As I approached her I noticed her eyes were totally white. I stopped and asked, "What's your name?" and she said she had no name. "May I give you a name?" I responded. At that point she started to laugh and I saw that she had two teeth—one hanging out, about to fall out. I said to her friend sitting beside her, "Does she have a name?"

She replied, "No, she's blind."

Well, surely she could still have a name, I'm thinking. I wrapped my arms around her and held her, rocking her. I said, "Your name is Uutolia. You exist with joy," and she started laughing again. And as I held Uutolia in my arms, God, my Father, Jesus, my Bridegroom King, Holy Spirit, my Comforter, turned her white eyes brown! Yes, Lord, the Healer!

Do you think for one moment that when I asked Uutolia if she wanted to know the Man who opened her eyes that she had a question? She said, "Where is He?"

I replied, "He's inside me and His name is Jesus." This thing called love is not that difficult when God's Presence goes with you.

We must want to learn His ways. We must want to learn the ways of His Presence. He's a Person who loves us and wants us to love Him. He's a Triune God—God the Father, God the Son, and God the Holy Spirit. We want to live in the Presence of the Person of God, to live in the Presence of the Person of Jesus. We want to live in the Presence of the Person, our Father. We want to be in the Presence of the Triune God.

PRESENCE PRAYER

Sweet Jesus, I want to love like You. Teach me what love looks like to You. I want to get lost in Your love. I want Your love to leak out of me. I need so much of Your love in me that it overtakes every part of me. Render me useless for anything that doesn't involve Your love.

SCRIPTURE REFLECTION

Read and reflect on Luke 6:35-36:

But love your enemies, do good to them, and lend to them without expecting to get anything back. Then your reward will be great, and you will be children of the Most High, because he is kind to the ungrateful and wicked. Be merciful, just as your Father is merciful.

This is not an easy Scripture to live out in real life. It sounds good when we read it, but reading and practical application are two different things. When you are faced with loving your enemies, come back to this Scripture and take hold of the promise of God found here: *"Then your reward will be great, and you will be children of the Most High."* What does it look like to be a son or daughter of the Most High?

Notes

Session

8

TO BE SATURATED BY GOD'S PRESENCE

Heidi Baker

SUMMARY

It is important for believers to have a dedicated, yielded time in the secret place. This is not a time when you're looking at your watch, trying to figure out what to do next. This is when you say to the Lord, "I must encounter Your Presence! I yield my mind, heart, emotions—my entire life to connect to You, the living God." This is the first step. When you take it, you will submerge into His Presence.

In Exodus 33, we find Moses in this place of utter yieldness.

As Moses went into the tent, the pillar of cloud would come down and stay at the entrance, while the Lord spoke with Moses. Whenever the people saw the pillar of cloud standing at the entrance to the tent, they all stood and worshiped, each at the entrance to their tent. **The Lord would speak to Moses face to face, as one speaks to a friend** (Exodus 33:9-11).

Did you catch that: "face to face, as one speaks to a friend"? Isn't that the best? Do you want a heart-to-heart conversation with God? Just yield completely to Him. Lay everything down and enter into His marvelous, holy Presence. There is nothing better this side of Heaven.

Living from His Presence is a lifestyle that requires a lifestyle of learning. God is a willing teacher. Place your hand in His hand and learn from Him. Jesus said, *"Take my yoke upon you and learn from me, for I am gentle and humble in heart, and you will find rest for your souls"* (Matt. 11:29).

INTERACTIVE QUESTIONS

1. In Day 1, Heidi speaks of "obedience to the Gentle Master." Jesus is our kind, tender Master—our sympathetic, benevolent, compassionate King. Why do you think it is so difficult for us to yield to Jesus when His nature is so loving and welcoming?

_____

_____

_____

_____

_____

2. God is calling you daily to press in to His Presence, and then press in more. Why? Why do you think God desires your presence?

_____

_____

_____

_____

_____

_____

_____

_____

3. Ananias, a disciple of Jesus in Damascus, was just a little piece of a big picture—a catalyst for God's Kingdom (see Acts 9:10-19). When God came with instructions to pray

for Saul, Ananias was so frightened by what he had heard about Saul that he really didn't want to do what God was asking of him, yet he obeyed. The result has impacted the world for Christ and His Kingdom in ways that Ananias never could have imagined. One would be led to believe that this seemingly insignificant disciple was living from God's Presence. How else would he have been able to overcome fear for his very life? Remember, Saul was having Christians killed. What has God called you to do that has made you fearful? Has your relationship with Him enabled you to overcome your fear, or not?

_____

_____

_____

_____

_____

_____

_____

4. It sounds so marvelous when Heidi says things like "living fully alive in His glory." How does this reconcile with the reality of holding a horribly disfigured child in your arms in a dirty street?

_____

_____

_____

_____

_____

_____

_____

_____

_____

5. What does Heidi means when she says, "He deals with His children differently than He deals with the rest of the world"?

_____

_____

_____

_____

_____

_____

_____

_____

_____

ACTIVATION EXERCISES

Group Activation

In this session, Heidi focuses on five ways in which we can be saturated in God's Presence—obedience, pressing in, being a catalyst for the Kingdom, living fully alive in His glory, and understanding our inheritance as believers. Think about which one or ones of these five you find easiest to do, and which one(s) are hardest. Share as you feel led.

Individual Activation

In this session, Heidi focuses on five ways in which we can be saturated in God's Presence—obedience, pressing in, being a catalyst for the Kingdom, living fully alive in His glory, and understanding our inheritance as believers. Which one or ones of these five do you find easiest to do, and which one(s) are hardest? How might you tackle the harder ones?

Day
1

OBEDIENCE TO THE GENTLE MASTER

*"Can anyone hide from me in a secret place? Am I not everywhere
in all the heavens and earth?" says the Lord.*
—JEREMIAH 23:24 NLT

THERE ARE NO SECRET PLACES APART FROM GOD, SO WHEN YOU SEEK HIM IN THE
secret place of His Presence, He will meet you there. In fact, He's already there waiting for you.

Once, I was scheduled to speak at a large convention in Asia. My hosts had gone to great lengths to welcome me and honor me. I was picked up at the airport in a black limo with tinted windows and booked into a five-star hotel. When I arrived, I heard the gentle Messenger, Holy Spirit, say, "Heidi, I need you to stay in your room."

"But, Lord," I said, "my hosts are not going to like that. They are not going to like it if I don't show up."

Again He said, "Heidi, I need to stay in your room and worship."

"Yes, Lord," I replied.

I called my hosts, who were wonderful people and had shown me such respect and provided me with everything of the best quality, and said, "I'm so sorry, but I have to obey God, and He told me to stay in my room and fast and pray until it is time for me to speak tonight." My hosts were surprised to say the least, and I could tell they weren't happy with my decision, but they graciously agreed.

In obedience to the gentle Messenger, I got on my knees and spent hours worshiping the Lord. I sang at the top of my lungs and was filled up and so full of joy. Then the flesh weaseled in for just a moment. "Shouldn't you look at the conference brochure?" said my flesh.

I kept worshiping, but I wanted to look at the brochure. The flesh kept nagging me until finally I looked. It was a four-color, stunning, slick brochure. I mean Asia slick, fantastic. I opened it and read through each section. When I got to the session that I told them I couldn't attend, I saw that pastors from twenty-some nations in Asia were coming for a lunch in my honor. It was to be a crazy awesome, huge Asian feast. My heart sank. Then I heard the Lord say, "Would you have had a different response to My request if you had looked the brochure first?"

I replied, "I wish I could say no, Lord, but I probably would have made myself go and made You wait and tried to squeeze time in with You before the next session." That was my honest answer, and I was sobbing as I spoke to the Lord. You see, we should never, ever choose people over God. When we are obedient to His leading, He will always lead us where we are meant to go. That day I was meant to spend time alone in the secret place with Him. I am so thankful I was obedient even though my flesh was weak.

PRESENCE PRAYER

Dear Lord Jesus, thank You that You don't ask anything of me that You Yourself have not experienced. I need You to help me overcome my flesh, for it is very weak! I am nothing without You, but with You all things are possible.

SCRIPTURE REFLECTION

Read Matthew 26:36-45. The weakness of our flesh is an affliction common to all. Think on the different ways you combat your flesh. Do any of them resemble Jesus' advice in verse 41?

Day
2

PRESS IN, PRESS IN, PRESS IN

THE LORD, KNOWING THE LOCAL CULTURE, KNOWING THE PEOPLE I HAD JUST offended, knowing what great expense they had borne, knowing how many people were involved and the distances they traveled—knowing all that, He said, "Don't worry about having missed the dinner. Just give them a tea."

"Give them a tea?" I responded. "What kind of a tea, Lord?"

"A five-star tea," was the response. Now, I am a missionary and I simply didn't have money for a five-star tea, and so I tried to argue just a little bit with God, but He wouldn't have it. He just kept instructing me to do a tea, and so I agreed with faith that He would provide.

When I spoke that evening, God crashed in. It was spectacular. Then, in front of about 8,000-10,000 people I said, "All missionaries and all pastors, I'm inviting you to tea tomorrow at my expense. I want to thank all of you. Holy Spirit told me I couldn't go to the banquet that was planned. I didn't know it was a banquet in my honor. Yet, I'm glad I didn't attend because I chose the right thing—His Presence—and so I hope you all can come tomorrow."

Later, I told the staff to go ahead and prepare for the tea. I spared no expense and told them to make it the best tea ever in Singapore—make delicious food, beautifully arranged with beautiful decorations. When I heard what the cost would be, I thought, *I've got to call Rolland. There's no way our debit card has that much in the account.* I'm thinking, *I'm a missionary. I feed the poor. Jesus, what are You thinking?* He said, "I'm God. You're not."

We had the tea, and everyone enjoyed it immensely. Afterward, somebody I didn't know handed me a fat envelope. He said, "The Lord said to give you this." When I opened the envelope and counted the money inside, it was the exact cost of that tea. The exact amount! That's living in the Presence. Do what He gives you to do and you will live in His Presence. You will pursue His Presence. You will encounter His Presence, and then you'll press in, press in, press in.

SCRIPTURE REFLECTION

Take time today in the Psalms, allowing them to lead you into the secret place. Psalms 42:1-2, 46:10, and 84:1-2 are good places to start.

BE A CATALYST FOR THE KINGDOM

IRIS HAS ONE OF HAVE THE MOST AMAZING TEAMS ON THE PLANET, AND I'M just one little person in that huge, amazing team of believers. One day I was talking to God in Mozambique, saying, "Lord, You told me to ask for a nation." When God says you can ask for a nation or a city, don't think you have to conquer it yourself. That would be insanity! Overwhelming insanity. You're just a little piece of the whole. But every piece matters in God's equation. I'm just a tiny little catalyst. You're a catalyst for the Kingdom too, and every catalyst for the Kingdom is important. Moses was a catalyst called to carry the glory—to carry the Presence.

> *Moses said to the Lord, "You have been telling me, 'Lead these people,' but you have not let me know whom you will send with me. You have said, **I know you by name***

and you have found favor with me.' If you are pleased with me, teach me your ways so I may know you and continue to find favor with you. Remember that this nation is your people" (Exodus 33:12-13).

Notice that Moses just assumes that he's not being called to lead alone. He knows he's a catalyst but not the only one. The Lord replied, *"My Presence will go with you, and I will give you rest"* (Exod. 33:14). What a gracious response from the Father. He will send His Presence when we ask Him, and no matter what issues we are facing, in His Presence we will find rest. Your life is in the hands of a loving God.

BIBLE STUDY

Read Matthew 4:17-25. Beginning in verse 17, Jesus makes the radical announcement that the Kingdom of Heaven has drawn near; it has arrived! The very next thing Jesus does is to begin calling His disciples. He gathers about Him a new community that operates on Kingdom values. Each member of this community (each disciple) will learn what it means to be a catalyst for the Kingdom. Jesus has called you. As you walk with Jesus, washing yourself in His Word and pressing into His Presence, how is He shaping you into a catalyst for His Kingdom?

Day
4

FULLY ALIVE IN HIS GLORY

YOU ARE NOT NAMELESS OR FACELESS. YOU WEREN'T CREATED JUST TO BRING glory to God. You were created because He loves you, and the fact that you acknowledge His love brings Him glory. In fact, it brings Him more glory than anything else you'll ever do. When you choose to live in His Presence, He's the happiest He could ever be with you. Do you want to live in His glory? Do you want to live in His Presence? You can—because He knows your name and everything else about you.

For years, Rolland and I picked up kids who were dying on the street. We used to be able to just say, "Hey, jump in our truck. Come live with us." No longer. Things have gotten complicated. One day we saw a dear little beggar boy whose face was horribly disfigured when a land mine went off right beside him. He had no eyes, half a mouth, no nose—just two little nostrils. He used to get quite a bit of money from begging because he was so terribly wounded. People called him the faceless boy. When I found him, I held him and rocked him in my arms, and the first thing I wanted to know was his name. Names matter. As I held him in my arms I called him Enoseao. I said, "Enoseao, you're beautiful. Enoseao, you exist. Enoseao, you have a name, and I see you." The land mine blew away his face, but he still had a name; he had value in the eyes of God.

You have a name, and Daddy God has a destiny for you. He wants you to live in His Presence. He wants you to be fully alive in His glory.

SCRIPTURE REFLECTION

Read Luke 19:37-38:

Then, as He was now drawing near the descent of the Mount of Olives, the whole multitude of the disciples began to rejoice and praise God with a loud voice for all the mighty works they had seen, saying: **"Blessed is the King who comes in the name of the Lord!"** *Peace in heaven and glory in the highest!"* (NKJV)

Jesus represents God, the King, the Lord Almighty. We are God's ambassadors to the world as well. How well are you representing King Jesus? Are you learning to live fully alive in His glory?

Day
5

THE INHERITANCE OF BELIEVERS

IT IS LIFE-CHANGING TO UNDERSTAND THE FULL FORCE OF WHAT IT MEANS TO be able to call the one true God our "Daddy" and what it means to be joint-heirs with Christ. Because of our relationship with God, we know He no longer deals with us as enemies; instead, we can approach a holy God as our heavenly Father with *"boldness"* (Heb. 10:19) and *"full assurance of faith"* (Heb. 10:22). We have that confidence because of the indwelling presence of the Holy Spirit who *"bears witness with our spirit that we are children of God, and if children, then heirs—heirs of God and joint-heirs with Christ, if indeed we suffer with Him, that we may also be glorified together"* (Rom. 8:16-17 NKJV).

The benefits of being adopted children of God are many. Becoming a child of God is the highest privilege and honor that can be imagined. Because of it we have a new relationship with

God and a new standing before Him. He deals with His children differently than He deals with the rest of the world. Being a child of God, adopted "through faith in Christ Jesus" is the source for our hope, the security of our future and the motivation to *walk worthy of the calling with which you were called"* (Eph. 4:1 NKJV). Being children of the King of Kings and Lord of Lords calls us to a higher standard, a different way of life and a greater hope.

As we come to understand the true nature of God as revealed in the Bible we should be amazed that He not only allows us, but even encourages us, to call Him "Abba Father." It is amazing that a holy and righteous God, who created and sustains all things, who is the only all-powerful, all-knowing, ever-present God, would allow sinful humans to call Him "Daddy." As we come to understand who God really is and how sinful we are, the privilege of being able to call Him "Abba Father" will take on a whole new meaning for us and help us understand God's amazing grace.

In Revelation 2:17, the Spirit announces that He will give a white stone with a new name written on it, known only to him who receives it. There is some disagreement as to the inter-pretation of this passage. One interpretation is that this new name is either given to the believer or God is revealing a new name for Himself that expresses a facet of His character not previously known. In either case, this new name is part of the inheritance of believers whom God has adopted into His family. We have been adopted by God and are His heirs according to Romans 8:17. As heirs, we are given insight by the Spirit into the grace and love of God and of Christ in us, the hope of glory. We have received a Spirit of adoption as sons and daughters by which we cry out, "Abba, Father!" What a great thing to be adopted by God! What a great privilege! What a marvelous inheritance! Through adoption we can come into a rich relationship with God, our loving heavenly Father.

God created us for His family. When we come home to the family of God, we come into Kingdom living where there is abundant joy and peace and hope. Home with God is a place where we are cherished and made whole. When you are home in God's embrace, you can saturate yourself in His presence until all of you is overcome by His great love.

PRESENCE PRAYER

Abba Father! I receive my adoption! I receive my inheritance! I want all You have for me. I want to be a yielded, laid-down lover of Your Presence at all times, everywhere, in all things. Thank You for Your sweet patience with me as I learn how to let go of the things of this world so that my heart has room to embrace the things of Your Kingdom. Thank You that You forgive me when I fail, help me up when I fall, love me when I am

unlovable so that I might help the fallen, forgive the failures, and love the unlovable—
to Your glory. Thank You, Jesus, that Your infinite worthiness covers my unworthiness.
How sweet it is to be a child of God.

SCRIPTURE REFLECTION

In the first chapter of the gospel of John, John the Baptist saw Jesus coming toward him and said, *"Look, the Lamb of God, who takes away the sin of the world!"* (John 1:29). In Jesus we have God's full and perfect provision. The breadth of this revelation is stunning. It goes beyond individual redemption to embrace the redemption of creation itself, rescuing it from the subjection of sin. You are part of this glorious liberty that belongs to the sons and daughters of God. How will you embrace this great gift that is Jesus? He longs for your answer.

Notes

ABOUT HEIDI AND ROLLAND BAKER

ROLLAND AND HEIDI BAKER, FOUNDERS AND DIRECTORS OF IRIS GLOBAL, HAVE served as missionaries for more than 35 years to the world's poorest people. Heidi earned her PhD degree at King's College, University of London, where the Bakers planted a thriving church for the homeless. Rolland has his Doctor of Ministry (D. Min.) from United Theological Seminary located in Dayton, Ohio. They have lived and ministered for the last 21 years in Mozambique. They also travel internationally, teaching about "passion and compassion" in the ministry of the Gospel. They have written several books, including *Always Enough, Expecting Miracles, Compelled by Love, Birthing the Miraculous, Reckless Devotion* and *Training for Harvest*.

FREE E-BOOKS?
YES, PLEASE!

Get **FREE** and deeply-discounted **Christian books** for your **e-reader** delivered to your inbox **every week!**

IT'S SIMPLE!

VISIT lovetoreadclub.com

SUBSCRIBE by entering your email address

RECEIVE free and discounted e-book offers and inspiring articles delivered to your inbox every week!

Unsubscribe at any time.

SUBSCRIBE NOW!

LOVE TO READ CLUB

visit **LOVETOREADCLUB.COM** ▶